Greenhill Books

SPEARHEAD
FOR
BLITZKRIEG

SPEARHEAD FOR BLITZKRIEG

LUFTWAFFE OPERATIONS IN SUPPORT OF THE ARMY, 1939–1945

General der Flieger Paul Deichmann
Edited and with an Introduction by
Dr Alfred Price

GREENHILL BOOKS, LONDON
STACKPOLE BOOKS, PENNSYLVANIA

Greenhill Books

Spearhead for Blitzkrieg
First published 1996 by Greenhill Books,
Lionel Leventhal Limited, Park House, 1 Russell Gardens, London NW11 9NN
and
Stackpole Books, 5067 Ritter Road, Mechanicsburg, PA 17055, USA

© Lionel Leventhal Limited, 1996
Introduction © Dr. Alfred Price, 1996

British Cataloguing in Publication Data available

ISBN 1-85367-241-6

Library of Congress Cataloging-in-Publication Data available

Publishing History
Spearhead for Blitzkrieg was originally published as *German Air Force Operations in
Support of the Army* (USAF Historical Studies No. 163), ed. Dr. Littleton B.
Atkinson, 1962, as part of The German Air Force Monograph Project of the
Historical Research Division, US Department of the Air Force.

Designed and typeset by Roger Chesneau
Printed and bound in Great Britain
by Bookcraft (Bath) Limited, Midsomer Norton

Contents

Illustrations

Foreword

TO THE ORIGINAL EDITION

Luftwaffe Operations in Support of the Army by General der Flieger Paul Deichmann is one of a series of studies written by, or based on information supplied by, former key officers of the German Air Force for the United States Air Force Historical Division. The purpose of the series is threefold:

1. to provide the United States Air Force with a comprehensive and, insofar as is possible, authoritative history of a major air force which suffered defeat in World War II;
2. to provide a history of that air force as prepared by many of its principal and responsible leaders;
3. to provide a first-hand account of that air force's unique combat in a major war with the forces of the Soviet Union.

This series of studies therefore covers in large part virtually all phases of the Luftwaffe's operations and organisation, from its camouflaged origin in the Reichswehr, during the period of secret German rearmament following World War I, through its participation in the Spanish Civil War and its massive operations and final defeat in World War II.

The German Air Force Historical Project (referred to hereafter by its shorter and current title, 'The GAF Monograph Project') has generated this and other specially prepared volumes which comprise, in one form or another, a total of more than 40 separate studies, some of them in multi-volume form. The project, which was conceived and developed by the USAF Historical Division, was, upon recommendation of Headquarters Air University late in 1952, approved and funded by Headquarters USAF in early 1953. General supervision was assigned to the USAF Historical Division by Headquarters USAF, which continued principal funding of the project through 30 June 1958. Within the Historical Division Dr. Albert F. Simpson and Mr. Joseph W. Angell, Jr., respectively, Chief and Assistant Chief of the Division, exercised overall supervision of the project. The first steps towards its initiation were taken in the fall of 1952 following a staff visit by Mr. Angell to the Historical Division, Headquarters United States Army, Europe, at Karlsruhe, Germany. There, the Army was conducting a somewhat similar historical project covering matters and operations largely of primary interest to that service. Whereas the Army's project had produced or was producing a multiplicity of studies of varying length and significance (more than 2,000 have been prepared by the Army project this far), early on it was decided that the Air Force should request a radically smaller number (less than fifty) which should be very carefully planned initially and rather closely integrated. Thirteen narrative histories of GAF combat operations, by theatre areas, and 27 monographic studies dealing with areas of particular interest to the United States Air Force were recommended to and approved by Headquarters USAF in the initial project proposal of late 1952.

By early 1953 the actual work of preparing the studies was begun. Colonel Wendell A. Hammer, USAF, was assigned as Project Officer, with duty station at the USAREUR Historical Division in Karlsruhe. General der Flieger Paul Deichmann was appointed and served continuously as Control Officer for the research and writing phases of the project; he also had duty station at the USAREUR Historical Division. Generalleutnant Hermann Plocher served as Assistant Control Officer until his recall to duty with the new German Air Force in the spring of 1957. These two widely experienced and high-ranking officers of the former Luftwaffe were secured as principal authors, or 'topic leaders', former officers of the Luftwaffe, each of whom, by virtue of his experience in World War II, was especially qualified to write on one of the topics approved for study. These 'topic leaders' were, in turn, assisted by 'home workers' – for the most part former general and field-grade officers with either specialised operation or technical experience. The contributions of these 'home workers', then, form the basic material of most of the studies. In writing his narrative, the 'topic leader' has put these contributions into their proper perspective.

In their authors' personal knowledge and experience these studies find their principal authority. Thus, they are neither unbiased nor are they 'histories' in the ordinary sense of that word. Instead, they constitute a vital part of the story without which the final history of Germany's role in World War II cannot be written.

In preparing these studies, however, the authors have not depended on their memories alone. For their personal knowledge has been augmented by a collection of Luftwaffe documents which has come to be known as the Karlsruhe Document Collection, now housed in the Archives Branch of the USAF Historical Division. This collection consists of directives, situation reports, war diaries, personal diaries, strength reports, minutes of meetings, aerial photographs and various other materials derived, chiefly, from three sources: the Captured German Documents Section of the Adjutant General in Alexandra, Virginia; the Air Ministry in London; and private German collections donated to the project by its participating authors and contributors. In addition, the collection includes the contributions of the 'home workers'. Thus, the interested researcher can test the conclusions of the 'topic leaders' against the basic documents or secure additional information on most of the subjects mentioned in the studies.

The authors have also made use of such materials as the records of the Nuremberg Trials, the manuscripts prepared by the Foreign Military Studies Branch of the USAREUR Historical Division, the official military histories of the United States and the United Kingdom, and the wealth of literature concerning World War II, both in German and English, which has appeared in book form or in military journals since 1945.

With the completion of the research and writing phases in 1958, the operations at Karlsruhe were closed out. At that time the project was moved to the Air University, Maxwell Air Force Base, Alabama, where the process of editing and publishing was begun under the editorship of Mr. Edwin P. Kennedy, Jr., with the overall supervision of Dr. Simpson.

The complexity of the GAF Monograph Project and the variety of participation which it has required can easily be deduced from the acknowledgements which follow. On the German side: General Deichmann, who, as Chief Control Officer, became the moving force behind the entire project, and his assistant, General Plocher; General Josef Kammhuber, a contributor to the project, who heads the new German Air Force, and who has consistently supported the project; Generaloberst Franz Halder, Chief of the German Army General Staff from 1938 to 1942, whose sympathetic assistance to the Project Officer, the Project Editor and the German Control Group was of the greatest value; the late Generalfeldmarschall Albert Kesselring, who contributed to several of the studies and who also, because of his prestige and popularity in German military circles, was able to encourage many others to contribute to the project; and all of the German 'topic leaders' and 'home workers' who are too numerous to mention here but whose names can be found in the prefaces and footnotes to the individual studies.

In Germany, Colonel Hammer served as Project Officer from early in 1953 until June 1957. Colonel Hammer's considerable diplomatic and administrative skills helped greatly towards assuring the project's success. Col. William S. Nye, USA, was Chief of the USAREUR Historical Division at the project's inception. His strong support provided an enviable example of interservice cooperation and set the pattern which his several successors followed.

In England, Mr. L. A. Jackets, Head of Air Historical Branch, British Air Ministry, gave invaluable assistance with captured Luftwaffe documents.

At the Air University, a number of people, both military and civilian, have given strong and expert support to the project. The several Commanders of Air University during the life of the project in Karlsruhe (1952–1958) without exception were interested in the project and give it their full backing. Other personnel at Headquarters Air University who have given freely of their time and experience include: the several Directors of the Research Studies Institute since 1952; Dr. James C. Shelburne, Educational Advisor to the Commander; Mr. J. S. Vann, Chief of Special Projects Branch, DCS/Operations; and Mr. Arthur F. Irwin, Chief, Budget Division, DCS/Comptroller.

The project is grateful to Lt. Col. Leonard C. Hoffmann, former Assistant Air Attaché to Germany, who gave indispensable aid during the project's last year in Germany. Also in Germany, Mr. Joseph P. Tustin, former Chief Historian of Headquarters, United States Air Forces in Europe, ably assisted the project by solving a variety of logistical and administrative problems.

Miss Sara E. Venable deserves special thanks for her expert typing of the manuscript.

The project is indebted to all the members of the USAREUR Historical Division, the Office of the Chief of Military History and the USAF Historical Division who, through direct assistance and advice, helped the project to achieve its goals.

Dr. Littleton B. Atkinson, who succeeded Mr. Kennedy as Project Editor in 1961, edited the manuscript for publication.

About the Author

General der Flieger Paul Deichmann was born in Fulda on 27 August 1898. Early in 1916 he entered the Imperial Army as a cadet in the 86th Regiment of Fusiliers, and was commissioned a Leutnant a week prior to his eighteenth birthday. In the following August he began service with flying units as an observer, and continued this duty to the end of the war. Towards the end of 1920 he transferred to the 3rd Prussian Infantry Regiment, and in April 1925 he was promoted to Oberleutnant. Having been temporarily released from the Army in 1928, he returned to active duty in 1931 with the 1st Infantry Regiment, and was promoted to Hauptmann in 1933. With the official establishment of the German Air Force in 1934, he entered the Reich Air Ministry. In April 1935 he was posted to the Luftwaffe General Staff, where in August of that year he was promoted to Major. In 1937 he received a unit command, II. Gruppe of Bomber Geschwader 253, and in 1938 he was promoted to Oberstleutnant.

In August 1940 he became Chief of Staff of Air Corps II. Two years later he attained the rank of Generalmajor, as Chief of Staff to the Air Commander-in-Chief South, Generalfeldmarschall Kesselring. By February 1943 he was Chief of Staff of Air Fleet 2, and in June of that year he assumed command of Air Division 1. In 1944 he was promoted to Generalleutnant and decorated with the Knight's Cross (the Ritterkreuz). At the end of the war he commanded Luftwaffe Command 4.

General Deichmann's contribution to the USAF German Air Force Historical Project was outstanding. In addition to the present monograph (and several supporting papers), he has also written monographs on the Luftwaffe methods of target analysis and weapons selection (both unpublished). As if this were not enough, especial recognition is due to General Deichmann for his outstanding contribution to the Project in his capacity as Control Officer from the inception of the program in 1953 to the termination of the writing phase of the Project in 1958.

Introduction
TO THIS EDITION

As stated in the Foreword, this work was part of a USAF historical project initiated in the 1950s to set down the lessons the Luftwaffe had learned at such great cost during World War II. The Luftwaffe was the only air force with extensive experience of combat against the Soviet armed forces. During 1941 and most of 1942 it had engaged its numerically superior opponent with considerable success, and the USAF was keen to learn how this was done. With the Cold War then in full swing, those lessons might still apply if the USA and the Soviet Union found themselves in a state of armed conflict. For their part, the ex-Luftwaffe senior officers were willing to assist their new ally in any way they could.

Drawing on his experiences during the campaign in Russia, the author described the types of air support operations that worked and, equally important, those that did not work. His conclusions are as valid today as they were in World War II. Ground-attack aircraft and bombers were (and still are) at their most effective when striking at compact and clearly defined targets. Almost by definition, that rules out camouflaged troops and vehicles dispersed over the battle area. If aircraft are sent against targets that are difficult to find or are unlikely to be destroyed by the weapons carried, no matter how desirable the destruction of those targets might be from the military standpoint, the chances are that the attack will be unsuccessful. The only time such chancy operations are justified is at a critical juncture in the land battle when one's forces are attacking or have come under heavy attack. Obviously, if aircraft are sent against targets in the battle area (which they have little chance of destroying), they are not hitting the types of targets they can destroy. In the enemy rear areas there were good targets aplenty – supply dumps, railway marshalling yards, troop concentrations. Further back lay the enemy armament factories. All these were left untouched if the aircraft had to concentrate their activities mainly in the battle area.

When they have to search for targets that are difficult to find, aircraft have no choice but to expose themselves to ground fire. As a result, losses will be heavier than those suffered in set-piece attacks on well-defined targets in the rear areas. Over Russia the Luftwaffe was bled white flying support missions for the Army. During the first hundred days of the campaign the Luftwaffe lost, on average, 16 planes destroyed and 10 damaged each day. That represented about 0.3 per cent of the sorties flown, a low attrition rate in percentage terms. Yet this was during a prolonged period of intensive air operations, and for the Luftwaffe the cumulative effect of those losses was disastrous.

Over the 100-day period the Luftwaffe lost more than 1,600 aircraft destroyed. A further 1,000 aircraft returned with major battle damage. That total of 2,600 aircraft destroyed or damaged was uncomfortably close to the 2,770 combat planes the Luftwaffe assigned to the campaign in the East when it opened. The German aircraft industry could not replace aircraft being lost at that rate. In July, August and September 1941 the factories delivered 2,179 new combat planes to the Luftwaffe. So the losses of aircraft destroyed and damaged *on the Eastern Front alone* exceeded production by about 20 per cent. Many of the damaged aircraft were repaired and returned to service, but the reserve of aircraft assembled before the campaign was rapidly exhausted.

By the end of October 1941 most Luftwaffe combat units on the Eastern Front had been in action without pause since the beginning of the campaign. Their equipment had suffered much wear and tear, deliveries of replacement aircraft no longer kept up with losses and many units were well below establishment. Even more serious in the long run, the reserve of trained crews that had sustained the Luftwaffe since the beginning of the war was exhausted. From now on the flow of replacement crews coming from the training units would be inadequate to keep pace with losses. Thus, as the author points out, the Luftwaffe exhausted itself during attacks on the wrong targets while failing to attack the right ones.

The author lays great stress on the effectiveness of operations against the enemy transport system, to seal off the battle area during a critical phase in the land battle. However, it is important to realise that during the early war period each of Germany's enemies was short of road transport. They had to rely on their rail network to move the bulk of their troops, equipment and supplies. By repeated air attacks it was possible to halt rail traffic in a limited area for a limited period of, say, five to ten days. Against enemies that were well supplied with road transport, as was the case later in the war, such disruption was far more difficult to achieve.

The author portrays well the feelings of hopelessness that started to grip the German forces on the Eastern Front from the beginning of 1943. No matter how many times they had floored their foe, he always picked himself up and seemed to return to the fight with even greater strength. The Russian numerical superiority had been expected, but from the mid-war period the Germans had to contend with an enemy that no longer fielded inferior equipment. In 1944 most German aircraft types used on the Eastern Front were developments of those that had fought over Poland in 1939. The Luftwaffe was expected to do ever more with ever less, until the front collapsed in Russia in June 1944. In fact the war in the East had already been lost a year earlier, and from then on the German defeat was only a matter of time.

One major area of disagreement this editor has with the author concerns the ability of aircraft to destroy enemy tanks after the mid-war period. The most-used Soviet tank, the T-34, was a well-armoured vehicle weighing 28 tons. Yet as a target for air attack it was extremely small – seen from above, its area was only 22 square yards. Against such a target the Luftwaffe found that its available bombs were almost useless. In general terms, any weapon powerful enough to destroy the T-34 (for example a bomb of 110lb or heavier) usually could not be delivered with sufficient accuracy to have much chance of scoring a direct hit. Conversely, any weapon accurate enough to hit the vehicle (for example a cannon of 20mm calibre or smaller) was not powerful enough to penetrate the armour. During the Battles of the Falaise Gap and 'The Bulge' in 1944, Allied fighter-bombers claimed large numbers of German tanks and armoured vehicles destroyed. Afterwards Allied investigation teams examined the wrecked tanks and armoured vehicles in these areas, to see how many had in fact been destroyed by air attack. The detailed reports on the two actions point to a high degree of overclaiming by pilots, with tank kills exaggerated by more than ten to one. The bombs and rockets used by the Allied fighter-bombers were powerful enough to destroy tanks if they hit them, but in truth these weapons were not accurate enough to score many hits. In the absence of such firm evidence regarding the success (or not) of German attacks on tanks on the Eastern Front, it is likely that there was a similar degree of overclaiming there also.

In his original text General Deichmann made several excellent points. These were probably lost to the general reader, however, due to the over-wordy translation into English. In re-editing and re-working this translation I have tried to make the text more readable. Where appropriate I have transposed sections of the text to place them in chronological or contextual order. I have also deleted sections which in my view did not contribute to an understanding of the subject. Where I felt it necessary to clarify parts of the original text, I have added a few words of my own [in square brackets]. In some areas my research leads me to conclusions which differ from those expressed by General Deichmann. Where I have felt it necessary to bring this to the reader's attention, I have set down my observations in the Chapter notes. To differentiate the references and comments in the original edition from those I have made, I have appended the latter 'A.P.'.

In this edition I have restored the original German ranks and also the unit designations of Staffel, Gruppe and Geschwader. The rank equivalents with those in the RAF and the USAAF and details of the structure of the German flying units are given in Appendices A and B respectively.

Dr. Alfred Price
Uppingham, Rutland, 1996

Part One

Establishing the Foundations

CHAPTER 1

German Experience of Air Support Operations Before World War II

Operational Experience during in World War I[1]
THE USE OF AIRCRAFT IN RECONNAISSANCE

In German Army exercises, aerial reconnaissance had proved its value as early as 1911. By the outbreak of war in 1914 that service had 33 Feldflieger Abteilungen (field air battalions) each with six aircraft and ten Festungsflieger Abteilungen (fortifications air battalions) each with four aircraft.

By the end of World War I the air reconnaissance forces belonging to the German Army had grown to include:

a. 31 Abteilungen with a total authorised strength of 90 Type C (two-seat) aircraft;
b. 99 Abteilungen with a total authorised strength of 705 Type C aircraft, including machines suitable for artillery reconnaissance and air photography;
c. 6 Abteilungen committed in Turkey, with a total authorised strength of 36 Type C aircraft.

Thus the reconnaissance units of the German Air Service had an authorised strength of 831 aircraft when the war ended.

By 1917 there was a basic doctrine for the employment of air reconnaissance units. Reconnaissance missions, both long-range and short-range, were usually flown by single aircraft. Air units flew a systematic programme of reconnaissance over the enemy rear areas, the aim being to furnish intelligence to support timely and effective counter-action against enemy moves, or assist with plans being prepared by the units' own command. Reconnaissance units were to furnish information on the following points:

a. movements in enemy rear areas;
b. the movement and assembly of enemy reserves, tanks and large cavalry forces;

c. the disposition of enemy artillery;

d. the movement of enemy assault troops into jumping-off positions;

e. the effective direction of friendly artillery fire;

f. the location of friendly front lines, during an advance or withdrawal.

The information furnished had to be confirmed by aerial photographs.

The Use of Aircraft in Air Combat

As early as the winter of 1914–15, the French had begun fitting machine guns to some aircraft, to prevent German reconnaissance planes executing their missions. At that time German aircraft carried only rifles and pistols and, no match for the new French aircraft, they suffered heavy losses.

A captured French aircraft[2] developed specifically for air-to-air combat provided the starting point for an innovation in aerial warfare. Inspired by the captured plane, Anthony Fokker designed a single-seat fighter monoplane with a single machine gun on a fixed mounting firing ahead through the propeller blades. This development created a new mission for the German Air Service: offensive combat action to achieve air superiority.

The fighter arm grew from about 40 aircraft in December 1915, to 81 fighter Staffeln with an authorised strength of between 1,134 and 1,926 aircraft by the war's end. Some Staffeln were consolidated into fighter Geschwader. When circumstances required, the fighters operated in small flights of two or three planes, in Staffeln of nine or ten planes, or in Geschwader with up to five Staffeln. In combat the advantage went to the airman who succeeded in attacking his opponent from above and from the rear, and pressed his attack to close range. Although units usually went into action in formation, once combat was joined the formation usually broke up and aircraft fought their own individual actions.

THE USE OF AIRCRAFT
FOR ATTACKING TARGETS IN THE ENEMY REAR AREAS

Before the war and during its early stages, trials were carried out using bombs to attack ground targets. Early types of bomb sight were also tested. At that time it was not possible to make systematic air attacks on targets, however.

In November 1914 the first unit was formed specifically to carry out bombing missions. Under the cover designation Brieftaubenabteilung Ostende (Carrier Pigeon Battalion Ostende), the unit came under the direct control of the Army High Command. Operating over Flanders, the unit received the best qualified pilots and observers available. The aircraft leading each formation was to carry an observer, while the rest flew as single-seaters and carried a correspondingly larger bomb load.[3]

By March 1915 the strength of the Bomber Geschwader had increased to six Staffeln each with six planes. To enable it to move quickly to areas of the heaviest fighting, it was assigned its own railway train. Sleeper carriages provided quarters for flying and ground personnel, there were freight trucks fitted out as workshops, and other trucks carried the unit's equipment, fuel and munitions. In April 1915 the unit transferred to Poland for operations on the Eastern Front. Based at airfields near Krakow, its aircraft provided support for German Army operations by attacking targets in the enemy rear area.

Gradually the bomber force expanded to five Geschwader, which were redesignated Bomber Geschwader of the Army High Command. There were also six independent bomber Staffeln. The first real successes by the new arm were achieved in 1916, following the entry into service of large [for those days] twin-engine bombers. From 1916 onwards, these units constituted the hard core of German bomber arm. On 13 June 1917 the 3rd GHQ Bomber Geschwader carried out the first large-scale bombing attack against London. Following this operation there were attacks on other targets in Britain.

Shortly before the war ended there were plans for an especially heavy attack against London, using several hundred thousand of the new 1kg (2.2lb) incendiary bombs.[4] The intention was to start major fires in the city. The Army High Command refused permission for the attack, however. It believed [probably correctly] that it would cause international outrage and do nothing to alter the deteriorating military situation facing Germany.

At the end of the war the Army High Command possessed eight bomber Geschwader with a total of 27 Staffeln and an authorised strength of 162 large aircraft. There were also two Abteilungen each with six super-large bombers.[5] These bombers were employed in strategic missions, for example against Britain, in which case their operations were independent of those carried out by ground forces. Elsewhere the large bombers operated against targets far behind the ground battle area. The ability of bomber units to move quickly between bases made it possible to concentrate forces as the situation required. By day, the bombers usually attacked in Geschwader or Staffel formations. If circumstances required, individual bombers sometimes flew attack missions, though this was not usual.

PARTICIPATION OF AIRCRAFT IN THE GROUND BATTLE

After the summer of 1916, reconnaissance aircraft carried a fixed machine gun firing forward and a flexible weapon in the observer's position firing to the rear. Following this development, it became common for aircraft flying at low altitude over enemy territory to engage ground targets with machine-gun fire. On occasions, good results were obtained during such actions. However, some time elapsed before special units formed to fly this type of mission.

On 10 July 1917, during an attack in Flanders, a bomber Staffel from one of the GHQ Geschwader provided close support for the infantry. The results, both in terms of the physical effects and the impact on enemy morale, were impressive. As a result the German High Command decided to employ the escort Staffeln, established in 1916 to provide protection for reconnaissance units, as ground support squadrons. The latter were to co-operate with the assaulting infantry by delivering attacks with bombs and machine gun on enemy artillery batteries and troops caught in the open.[6]

Since the mission of these ground support units was to participate in ground combat, they were to go into action the moment the infantry forces left their trenches. The intention was to bring movement into what had become a static war. At such a time enemy machine guns which might have been a threat to the low-flying aircraft were occupied in engaging the attacking infantry. Ground-attack aircraft struck at enemy positions holding up the advancing infantry. When possible other types of aircraft, including fighters, bombers and reconnaissance planes, would also participate in the land battle. The basic principle was that every aircraft that could carry bombs and machine guns should assist the advancing infantry.

The following maxim, dating from 1916, best describes the degree of cooperation that existed between the Air Service and the Army in World War I (and in World War II): no battle on the ground should be fought without the Air Service making its honourable contribution.

At the end of the war the German Air Service had more than 38 ground-support Staffeln with an authorised strength of 228 aircraft.

Command Control of the Air Force in World War I

During this conflict the Air Service and the anti-aircraft artillery forces were an organic part of the Army. Yet it had soon become evident that a separate command organisation was necessary, to control these forces and coordinate their activities with those of the Army.

In a Cabinet Order dated 8 October 1916, responsibility for the 'uniform development, readiness and employment' of the means of air combat and air defence was assigned to a Commanding General of Air Service. This officer was subordinated to the Chief of the Army General Staff (Chef des Generalstabes des Feldheeres). At each field army head-quarters was a Commander of Tactical Support Air Units (Kommander der Flieger) and his staff, to oversee the provision of air support for that army. At an important sector of the battle front, an air commander was attached to the appropriate corps headquarters. Also, air liaison officers were attached to other corps headquarters and to divisional staffs.

Recommendations to Establish
the Air Force as a Separate Service

Early in 1916 the Field Air Commander submitted to the Chief of the Army General Staff a plan calling for the consolidation of all fighter and bomber units into what was to be called the Imperial Air Force. The aim was to have a single command agency to control the organisation, training, administration and operations of the combat forces. This would make the Air Force a third and separate service, alongside the Army and the Navy. General von Falkenhayn, Chief of the Army General Staff, approved its recommendations and supported the plan wholeheartedly. Political considerations prevented the plan from being implemented, however. Several German states had raised their own air contingents, and they thought that the formation of such a unified air force would infringe their sovereign rights. The best that could be done was to establish unified operational control of flying units, under the Commanding General of the Air Service. As mentioned earlier, this was instituted in October 1916. On 1 April 1918 Great Britain created the Royal Air Force as a separate service, but another eighteen years would elapse before Germany adopted such a system.

The Impact of the Treaty
of Versailles on the German Air Forces

At the time of the Armistice in November 1918 the German Air Service comprised 290 Staffeln with a total authorised strength of 2,709 aircraft of all types. The force had a strength of 4,500 officers, noncommissioned officers and men.

The war had shown the importance of having an air force to support land operations. Yet although the Treaty of Versailles allowed a standing

German Army of 100,000 officers and men, it forbade any air contingent. To provide for one when this ban was lifted, the Chief of the German Army Command ordered that a number of well-qualified air officers be placed in staff positions in the new Army. Later, this wise move would reap its reward in providing a high degree of cooperation achieved between the Army and new Air Force.[7]

Provisions in the New Army
for Future Establishment of an Air Component
PREPARATORY PLANNING, 1926–1933

Even during the period when the new German Army was allowed no aircraft, the armed forces continued to study concepts of aerial warfare. All new plans took into account the mission of the Air Force in an armed conflict. As early as 1926 the Reichswehrministerium, the ministerial department for military affairs, issued a memorandum on the subject entitled 'Directives for the Conduct of Operational Aerial Warfare'. Since the German military forces had no aircraft, the memorandum bore the subtitle 'Compiled from Publications of Foreign Air Forces'. In reality, however, the memorandum represented the then-current German views on the employment of a modern air force. Later the memorandum was supplemented by a series of pamphlets describing the various missions that air elements would be required to undertake. The pamphlets were stapled into a hardback cover, allowing the insertion of new or updated pamphlets as these became available. Because of its colour the book became known as the 'Green Mail' (Gruene Post), a pun on a similarly titled German farming weekly. Following the establishment of the Air Ministry in 1934, a special staff under General Helmuth Wilberg[8] prepared an official manual on air operations. Entitled 'The Conduct of Air Operations' (Luftkriegfuehrung), Air Field Manual No. 16 appeared in 1935.[9] The manual contained the doctrine regarding cooperation between the Air Force and the Army. Moreover, the principles expounded in the manual determined the organisation of the new German Air Force. With minor changes, the manual established the ground rules for the conduct of Luftwaffe operations when World War II began.

MISSIONS FOR THE PLANNED NEW GERMAN AIR FORCE

Air Field Manual No. 16 set out the following missions for the newly formed Luftwaffe:

a. action to secure and maintain air superiority (this was considered a continuing mission, even when the Luftwaffe devoted attention to other types of operation);

b. action in support of the ground forces;

c. action in support of the Navy or the conduct of an air war independently at sea;

d. action to interdict enemy lines of communication such as road, rail and waterway routes, leading to or from the battle area or used to move imports or supplies;

e. strategic operations against sources of hostile military power;

f. attacks against targets in large cities, for example enemy centres of government and administration, and military control and training centres (in certain circumstances, retaliatory attacks might be carried out on enemy cities).

From the above it can be seen that the provision of air support for the Army was but one of several missions the Luftwaffe was to undertake. However, in securing and maintaining air superiority, attacking enemy communications or accomplishing its other missions, the Luftwaffe would provide indirect support for Army operations.

ARMY SUPPORT AS A MISSION OF AIR POWER

It was only natural that the Army should expect maximum air support. Also, given the increased capabilities of new aircraft types, the nature and scope of the support expected was far greater than that given in World War I. In the view of the Army, aircraft were particularly useful for transporting combat personnel in the execution of certain types of mission. The large carrying capacities of the latest aircraft made it possible to transport troops and supplies speedily over long distances. They could also move weapons, to develop concentrations speedily at critical points. Aircraft were invaluable for providing visual and photographic reconnaissance. Aircraft could also attack moving targets that otherwise could not be engaged by aimed fire from the ground. With their relatively long range, aircraft could attack targets in the rear areas beyond the artillery range. They were also useful for providing courier services to transport important personnel, documents and material.

As World War I had shown, fighters were the most effective means of combating hostile aircraft. They could prevent effective air reconnaissance by the enemy, thereby protecting friendly ground forces from observation. Also, they could prevent enemy air attacks on friendly ground forces. This feeling of security from air attack increased the combat efficiency of ground troops. Furthermore, when troops saw aircraft attacking enemy positions in front of them, it raised their combat morale in a way that could not be achieved by other means. Often this improvement in morale far outweighed the material results achieved by the air attacks.

To sum up, the following missions had been evolved for air power in support of the Army:

    a. the conduct of air reconnaissance;

    b. action to protect ground troops and installations from enemy air reconnaissance and air attack;

    c. support of the Army with attacks on ground targets;

    d. air transport, liaison and courier services.

Of these missions, the first two were seen as continuing tasks of the air forces, whereas the last two were tasks to be performed as and when required.

Thus, the essential problems facing the Luftwaffe in its future development became evident. The re-established Luftwaffe melded past experience with its existing and envisaged future capabilities. In this way it would determine the ways to accomplish its numerous missions and, if required, render the Army maximum support.

Notes to Chapter 1

1. The material for this chapter has been taken largely from *Handbuch der neuzeitlichen Wehrwissenschaften* (Manual for Modern Military Science), Karlsruhe Document Collection, G X 1, 1939.

2. The captured French plane was a Morane-Saulnier 'N' scout, with a Lewis gun mounted so as to fire through the propeller. In order to prevent bullets damaging the propeller, triangular metal deflector plates were fastened to each blade. Faced with a revolution in aerial warfare as represented by this simple but effective French device, the German authorities called in Anthony Fokker to design a similar device. From the French improvisation Fokker conceived the idea of a machine gun synchronised to fire through the propeller, thus eliminating the deflector plates. Henri Hegener,*Fokker – The Man and the Aircraft*, Harleyford Publications (Letchworth, England, 1961) pp. 24–5.

3. The unit operated some thirty aircraft, LVG, Aviatik and Albatros B-1 single-engine, two-seat biplanes. The bomb load carried depended on the distance to the

target, but was typically about 150lb. Rarely did the attacks cause damage of military significance. Bomb sights were rudimentary and, as a result, the bombing was inaccurate. Moreover, the small bombs used had limited explosive power, poor ballistics and unreliable fusing. The science of aerial bombing was still in its infancy and this would remain the case until the late 1930s.—A.P.

4. This incendiary bomb was named after the German company that made it, Elektron.

5. Typical of the twin-engine bombers was the Gotha G.IV, which carried a crew of three and up to 660lb of bombs. Typical of the super-large bombers was the four-engine Staaken R.VI, which carried a crew of between five and seven and a bomb load of 3,960lb.—A.P.

6. Following the large-scale British tank attack and breakthrough during at Cambrai in November 1917, the German Air Service redeployed several specialised ground attack units to support the land battle. The aircraft, Halberstadt CL II and Hannover CL III two-seat biplanes, made low-level attacks with machine guns and hand-dropped grenades. These were effective against British troops moving in the open, and they delayed the advance and gave time for German ground forces to re-establish the defensive line. Since there was no armour protection for the crews, however, these units suffered heavy losses. In the spring of 1918 the Junkers J-1 armoured ground attack aircraft entered service, with sheets of 5mm armour plate protecting the engine and two-man crew. Neither the Allied front-line troops nor the Allied fighter aircraft possessed automatic weapons heavier than rifle calibre, so these aircraft could operate over the battle area with relative impunity. Armed with two machine guns operated by the observer, they flew low to attack enemy troops caught in the open and were highly effective. The disadvantage of these unwieldy and slow aircraft was that they could be used effectively only during major land actions, in the brief periods when enemy infantry left the protection of their trenches.—A.P.

7. The number of experienced air officers was insufficient, however, for the needs of the Luftwaffe when it was re-established in the 1930s. Albert Kesselring, *Kesselring: A Soldier's Record* (New York, 1954), p. 23. See also Richard Suchenwirth, *Historical Turning Points in the German Air Force War Effort*, USAF Historical Studies No. 89, pp. 1–2, 15–16.

8. General der Flieger Wilberg was killed in an accident in 1941. He had served in World War I as Chief of Tactical Air Command, German Fourth Army, which was committed in the area of main effort in the Western Theatre.

9. Hereafter referred to as Air Field Manual No. 16.

CHAPTER 2

Putting Theory into Practice

Relations Between an Independent Luftwaffe and the Army
FORMULATING THE MISSION OF THE NEW LUFTWAFFE

In establishing the new German Luftwaffe in 1934, the High Command followed a course similar to that suggested by the Field Air Commander in 1916. The aim was to consolidate all elements operating in the air to create an Air Force as a third branch of the armed forces. No evidence has been found to connect the 1916 plan with the one that came to fruition in 1934. Nevertheless, it can be assumed that those who advised on the development of the new Luftwaffe had the 1916 plan at the back of their minds. The new plan went further, however, by including in the Air Force the anti-aircraft artillery forces intended 'for action against targets in the air'.

Those who defined the mission of the new Luftwaffe were well aware of the capabilities and limitations of air power. They took the line that the new independent Luftwaffe could not, alone, secure a decision, leaving the Army and Navy to carry out defensive missions. On the contrary, the Luftwaffe was to serve under the Joint Armed Forces High Command, operating with the Army and Navy 'to break the combat power of hostile military forces'. Air Field Manual No. 16 set out the main principles of the mission of the Luftwaffe in the clearest of terms:

> The mission of the Armed Forces in war is to break the will of the enemy.
> The will of a nation finds its strongest expression in the nation's military forces. Defeat of the enemy military forces is the primary objective in war.
> The mission of the Luftwaffe is to serve this purpose by conducting air warfare as part of the overall pattern for the conduct of the war.
> In war victory can be secured only through the combined efforts of all three branches of the military forces.
> By coordinating the operations of the Army, the Navy and the Luftwaffe, and through shifts in emphasis in the military forces, the Supreme Command endeavours to achieve maximum effectiveness.

From the above statements it is clear that the Luftwaffe was to act as part of a joint military effort. For the Luftwaffe to secure victory alone, without support from the other two services, it would have required far greater strength. Due to the limited resources available to the German government, such an increase in Luftwaffe strength would have been possible only at the expense of the Army and the Navy.

It was foreseen, however, that in war a situation could arise where a change in the balance of the forces might be the only means of achieving victory. Accomplishing such a change would not be easy, however. It would require the use of raw materials, machine tools and manpower on a large scale. Moreover, the training programmes would have had to be expanded to meet the new requirements. This would have taken several years. Air Field Manual No. 16 mentioned the possibility that such a situation might arise:

> If operations on the ground come to a stalemate, the Luftwaffe might be the only service capable of preventing the ground forces being bled white and the only means of securing victory. In that case the primary condition for success would be a shift in emphasis towards air warfare, at the expense of other means of waging war. Such a change in the conduct of war takes time and, as a precaution, preparations should be made well in advance.

Towards the end of the 1940 campaign in France Adolf Hitler considered this course. For a time he contemplated disbanding twenty army divisions, to release workers for the aircraft industry so that the Luftwaffe could be expanded to secure victory against Britain operating alone. However, the idea never progressed beyond the discussion stage.

Concentration of Air Power

It was only natural that the Army and Navy High Commands should demand combat air units of their own that were separate from those of the Luftwaffe. Because of limited resources, however, it was decided at the highest level that there should be a single, uniformly controlled Air Force. This would provide the necessary air support for the Army and Navy. Past experience had shown that subdividing an air force, particularly its combat elements, resulted in a dispersion of effort. This would nullify the flexibility, mobility and ability to redeploy swiftly, the very factors that make air power such a potent force.

The advantages of air power could be exploited only by concentrating forces at the point of decision. Such concentrations could be assembled rapidly in widely separated areas, as dictated by the military situation. Only by such means could the Luftwaffe commit the bulk of its forces to support individual armies, to secure victory or save ground forces from threatened destruction.

Development of the Command Organisation

Since the Army and the Navy could not have their own air units, and since the Luftwaffe had several missions to execute, an impartial command authority was necessary at a level higher than the three branches of the armed forces. This headquarters would decide the type, scope, and duration of support the Luftwaffe would provide when meeting requests from the other two services. Air Field Manual No. 16 provided for this contingency in paragraph 11:

> How the most effective results can be obtained, and which missions should receive priority, can be decided only by considering the entire military situation. Only after careful consideration of all relevant factors can the most important objectives be determined.

The supreme command authority of the German military forces was the Wehrmacht High Command (Oberkommando der Wehrmacht, the OKW). Concerning its responsibilities, Air Field Manual No. 16 observed:

> In such cases the Commander-in-Chief of the Wehrmacht will coordinate the army's requirements with those of the Luftwaffe, to determine the proportion of Luftwaffe forces to be committed to supporting ground operations.[1]

To carry out High Command directives regarding the provision of air support for the army, the Luftwaffe established a centralised command authority to issue the necessary orders. The latter defined the type and scope of the air support to be provided, and detailed the forces assigned for the purpose. Having received its directives, the Luftwaffe High Command had to liaise with the Army High Command to decide how best to employ units to support the ground forces.

Luftwaffe Higher Field Commands
to Provide Air Support for the Army

Under the Luftwaffe High Command, two types of Luftwaffe headquarters existed to provide air support for the Army:

    1. Luftwaffe headquarters assigned to Army commands

        These headquarters controlled only those air and anti-aircraft artillery units allocated to them, and came under the tactical control of the Army.

The assignment of Luftwaffe commands to the Army was in line with their organisation in World War I, when the following posts had existed:

a. An Air Service General attached to the Commander-in-Chief of the Army;

b. a Commander of Tactical Air Support Forces assigned each army group and army level headquarters; and

c. air liaison teams or air liaison officers attached to army corps or divisions operating in areas of main effort. These officers served as advisors at the appropriate army commands, and exercised administrative and disciplinary control over Air Service units allocated to the Army.

Army officers tended to regard aircraft as a means of transportation, to move observers, cameras or weapons about as required. The Luftwaffe, in contrast, held the view that the employment of aircraft was subject to special conditions. They were unlike any of the other weapons used by the other two services. The differing capabilities of the various categories of aircraft, differences in the capabilities of crews, the influence of weather and the speed with which the air situation could change – these and other factors meant that only appropriately trained Luftwaffe officers should direct air operations. Because of this, even those Luftwaffe units assigned permanently to the Army were directed from headquarters staffed by Luftwaffe personnel. Under this arrangement Luftwaffe units belonged to the Army only to the extent that the appropriate army headquarters allocated their operational missions. The Luftwaffe headquarters was responsible for deciding the manner in which a mission was flown.

In 1942 the Luftwaffe headquarters assigned to army commands were deactivated and their mission was reassigned to the headquarters of the operational air forces. The purpose of the change was to economise in manpower. By then cooperation between the operational air forces and the army commands was so close that it was thought that the step would have no ill effects. The various Air Fleets attached air liaison teams to the army group and army headquarters.

2. *Higher-level Luftwaffe headquarters*

These headquarters furnished temporary support to the Army, while executing their other missions. To ensure that only one Luftwaffe headquarters worked with any one army group headquarters, the operational boundaries of Air Fleets coincided with those of the army groups.

At the level of the field army, it was not possible to link zones of air operations to the zones of operation of individual armies. That would have caused too great a dispersion of Luftwaffe forces, and it ran contrary the principle of concentrating air power for maximum effect. Individual air units were therefore assigned to support the individual armies of the army group concerned. Such missions were assigned to Air Corps and Air Divisions, or to lower air commands if the situation required.

Luftwaffe Forces Allocated Permanently to the Army

According to directives from the Wehrmacht High Command, air support was primarily the responsibility of the operational air forces. As we have seen, up to 1942 air units were assigned permanently to the Army. Air Field Manual No. 16 provided for this in paragraph 121:

> Direct cooperation with and direct support for the Army are the primary missions of Luftwaffe units allocated to the Army for reconnaissance and air defence purposes. The forces in question include reconnaissance, anti-aircraft artillery, aircraft reporting and, if the situation requires it, fighters.

Accordingly, long-range and short-range reconnaissance units, anti-aircraft artillery and aircraft reporting companies came under Army command. Fighter units were not assigned in this way, however. As pointed out earlier, the system of placing Luftwaffe units under Army control ceased in 1942. From then on, all such units were assigned to Air Force commands which employed them as previously in support of the Army.

Development, Production
and Use of Tactical Reconnaissance Aircraft

At the outbreak of war the Army had control of thirty tactical, or short-range, air reconnaissance Staffeln. One such unit was assigned to each of its corps, for tactical and battle reconnaissance and artillery spotting.

At the start of the Russian campaign in 1941 there were 36 tactical air reconnaissance squadrons, each with seven aircraft. In addition there were twenty Staffeln, each with six aircraft, for assignment to major armoured units. In succeeding years the tactical reconnaissance force remained relatively stable, with a monthly average of twenty-nine Staffeln in 1942, thirty-two in 1943 and thirty in 1944.

Among the aircraft types developed by the Reichsheer (German's post-World War I, 100,000-man army) under the difficult conditions following the Treaty of Versailles were the Heinkel 45 and Heinkel 46 reconnaissance planes.[2] The He 46 had been designed in 1930 to meet a Reichsheer specification for a tactical reconnaissance aircraft. Its rugged construction allowed it to operate from field airstrips, and the high-set wing afforded the crew a good field of vision. It entered production in 1933, but by 1939 its speed, radius of action and operating altitude were inadequate for tactical reconnaissance missions. It was vulnerable to battle damage and the lack of armour limited its usefulness. Moreover, the plane was not equipped for bad-weather or night operations. Because of these weaknesses the He 46 saw only limited use.

The He 45 biplane was also designed in 1930, to meet a Reichsheer specification for a long-range reconnaissance plane and light bomber. It also entered production in 1933. As early as 1935 it was clear that its radius of action was inadequate for operations with mobile ground forces. The aircraft were transferred to the tactical reconnaissance Staffeln, which received three each. Even as a tactical reconnaissance aircraft, however, the He 45 was barely adequate for the Polish campaign. Like the He 46, it was vulnerable to battle damage, it had inadequate defensive armament and it was not equipped for night or bad-weather operations.

In 1939 most [tactical reconnaissance] Staffeln had three He 45s and six He 46s, plus another three He 46s in reserve. Although outdated, these machines served in front-line units and participated in the Polish campaign. In addition, each Staffel had three Fieseler 156 Storch liaison planes and a Junkers W 34 or a similar light transport aircraft.

Designed to replace the He 46, the Henschel 126[3] entered production in 1938. In contrast to the He 45 and He 46, which were of mixed steel, wood and fabric construction, the all-metal Hs 126 had the advantage of being weather-resistant. Protective shelters were unnecessary, and this facilitated the aircraft's camouflage in open terrain. The speed and climbing performance the Hs 126 were superior to those of the He 45 and the He 46. The fuel tank had armour protection, making the new aircraft less vulnerable to enemy fire. During the Polish campaign additional armour was fitted to protect the pilot and observer from rounds fired from the rear [i.e., from enemy fighters]. The crew had no protection against ground fire, however. The weapons carried by the Hs 126 were the same as those carried by the earlier types, and its defensive armament was still inadequate. The Hs 126 had provision to carry navigational and radio equipment to permit night and bad-weather operations. To sum up, the Hs 126 was a rugged, reliable, weatherproof plane well able to undertake the tactical and battlefield reconnaissance mission.

At the outbreak of war there were sufficient Hs 126s to equip only some of the tactical reconnaissance Staffeln in the Polish campaign. Not until the 1940 were there enough of these aircraft to equip all of the tactical reconnaissance units. The aircraft fulfilled the needs of the Polish campaign and those in the West and in the Balkans. From mid-1941, however, it was no longer suitable for operations in areas where it might encounter modern enemy fighters.

Production of the Hs 126 failed to meet demand, and during the Russian campaign the strength of tactical Staffeln dropped from nine aircraft to seven. Staffeln assigned to Panzer divisions each had six aircraft. The requirement for each Staffel to hold three aircraft in reserve had to be suspended. During the latter half of 1941 production still failed to keep up with losses and the tactical reconnaissance force declined in strength. By the end of the year the average strength of Staffeln operating with Army Group South [for example] had fallen to a single serviceable aircraft.

One reason why tactical reconnaissance aircraft were not developed as energetically as other military types was that, before the war, the main effort was directed to building combat forces to deter war.[4] Another was that, until a few months before the invasion of Poland, Hitler had assured his military commanders that there would be no war before 1942. Yet another reason for the neglect of tactical reconnaissance was that during the military build-up there was no army authority with the necessary powers of command. Such an authority was established only in March 1939, as the Commander of Army Air Forces and Luftwaffe General Attached to the Commander-in-Chief of the Army. The latter controlled all long-range and short-range air reconnaissance units allocated to the Army. Before that, units were grouped together under the operational air forces. Naturally, these headquarters took less interest in those units they would not control in war than their own bomber and fighter units.

The Inspectorate of Air Reconnaissance Forces and Air Photography was responsible for supervising air reconnaissance units. This section also produced specifications for new reconnaissance aircraft. Whether these requirements were to be met rested with the Luftwaffe General Staff, however. The latter weighed these requirements with those from competing Inspectorates, for example those overseeing the development of bombers and fighters, before reaching a decision.

The difficulties encountered by the Inspectorate of Air Reconnaissance Forces are illustrated by the case of the Focke Wulf 189.[5] This aircraft was developed to a specification issued by the Inspectorate in 1937, and it was ready for series production by the end of that year. Yet as late as June 1939 the Luftwaffe General Staff refused to approve production because the aircraft was not fast enough. The FW 189 was a considerable improvement over the older types and, being a twin-engine aircraft, it had a greater safety factor. It carried a third crew member to act as rear gunner, which relieved the observer of this function and provided constant observation in that quarter. The observer sat beside the pilot, which made for a good understanding between them. The enclosed cabin afforded greater protection [from the weather] and allowed the crew greater freedom of movement. The extensive glazing round the cabin gave both the pilot and the observer an excellent field of view ahead and below, which was particularly useful during photographic sorties. When carrying radio equipment and a radio operator (who also served as rear gunner) the FW 189 had a full blind-flying capability. Of the tactical reconnaissance aircraft used by the Luftwaffe, the FW 189 was nearest to the ideal. It was superior to all previous types in its construction, its facilities for crew cooperation, its armament, its equipment and its operating range. Its main disadvantage was that it was no faster than the Hs 126.

In the end the FW 189 entered production as a successor to the Hs 126, but by then much time had been lost. At the start of the Russian campaign in June 1941 few FW 189s were in service with tactical reconnaissance squadrons. Throughout 1942 the plane was considered suitable in every respect for short-range and battlefield reconnaissance missions. Once the Russian fighter force started to improve, however, the relatively slow FW 189 no longer fulfilled the requirement. Thereafter the type was relegated to the night reconnaissance role, in which it served until the end of the war.

It may be asked whether it was wise to try to incorporate the separate missions of tactical, battlefield and artillery reconnaissance in the same type of aircraft. Certain aspects of these missions required widely different features. For the tactical reconnaissance role the aircraft had to undertake a mission similar to that flown by the strategic reconnaissance units. It could be therefore be argued that up to half of the planes in a tactical reconnaissance Staffel should have been twin-engine strategic reconnaissance aircraft. Not only would such aircraft have been more suitable for the normal tactical missions but they could also have flown the longer range missions.

Battlefield reconnaissance required an aircraft with armour protection, which could probably also have served as a ground-attack plane. A plane of this type could also have handled the short range artillery reconnaissance missions. Technically, such an armoured battlefield reconnaissance plane could have been built, since the German Air Service had operated such aircraft in 1918.

It is also possible that helicopters could have performed the short-range artillery reconnaissance mission better than fixed-wing aircraft. Before the war the artillery arm made repeated requests for helicopters to replace the tethered observation balloons then in use. However, the Luftwaffe High Command refused to introduce helicopters for artillery spotting, although a suitable type [the Focke-Achgelis 61] was available before the war.[6]

The artillery arm also requested that the short take-off and landing Fieseler 156 Storch liaison plane be used for reconnaissance and directing gunfire. However, the Inspector of Air Reconnaissance Forces refused this request, stating that it was too slow and could not be employed without fighter protection. The number of Fieseler Storch aircraft lost in forward areas during liaison missions confirmed this view.

Finally, the question should be addressed why the use of single-seater fighter aircraft for reconnaissance missions was not considered earlier. This was first suggested to the Inspector of Air Reconnaissance Forces in the winter of 1939–40 by the Luftwaffe Operations Staff. The Inspector considered that fighter aircraft would be suitable only for tactical air reconnaissance photography missions, but not for tactical battlefield reconnaissance or artillery reconnaissance. Since more powerful engines were not available for the FW 189, and there was no other suitable aircraft in prospect, it became necessary to employ fighter-type aircraft in the reconnaissance role. To this end the Messerschmitt 109G and the Focke Wulf 190A-6 were modified for this purpose.

At first it was thought that the disadvantage of having no observer could be accepted only on special reconnaissance missions. However, developments in foreign countries indicated that the modified fighter-type aircraft could perform the reconnaissance role. The performance of the fighter-reconnaissance aircraft was far superior to that of any multi-seat reconnaissance type. Moreover, it could defend itself, and due to its greater speed and manoeuvrability it could avoid anti-aircraft fire more easily than normal reconnaissance types. Finally, its excellent performance in the dive enabled it to descend swiftly to observe detail on the ground, then zoom quickly back to altitude.

The fighter-reconnaissance plane also had distinct disadvantages, however. Its pilot had perform the task of observer in addition to his normal tasks. It could carry out road reconnaissance, but not a point reconnaissance mission (for example, to determine the precise location of an enemy battery). Artillery observation was also a difficult mission: it was impossible to observe accurately the fall of artillery fire without having an observer for that purpose. A single-seater could carry out vertical air photography, but it was impossible to take the oblique photos necessary for battlefield reconnaissance [*sic*, but see note 7]. The photography of large areas, for map-making (for example, where accurate lateral overlapping of cover is necessary), was another mission a single-seater could hardly be expected to fulfil. Such missions had to be assigned to long-range reconnaissance units. For bad-weather and night missions the usefulness of the reconnaissance fighter was limited. In poor visibility the pilot had to concentrate on flying the plane, which lessened or prevented tactical observations. Despite these limitations, however, single-seaters were able to carry out most types of tactical reconnaissance mission.

Strategic Reconnaissance Units Operating with the Army

From July 1934, the initial equipment of the newly formed long-range reconnaissance squadrons was the Heinkel 45. In view of the inadequacies of this aircraft, in the following year each long-range reconnaissance Staffel received three Heinkel 70 aircraft. The He 70 was a fast, single-engine monoplane [it was originally designed for Lufthansa as a high-speed mail carrier]. For the long-range reconnaissance role it was fitted with a defensive armament and other military equipment. Yet, in spite of its advantage of speed over the He 45 [about 45mph], the He 70 was of limited value for long-range reconnaissance [mainly on account of the poor field of vision from the observer's position].

In 1937 the Dornier 17P began to equip the long-range reconnaissance Staffeln allocated to the Army. This twin-engine aircraft rendered excellent service. During the campaigns in Poland and France the Luftwaffe assigned ten long-range or strategic air reconnaissance Staffeln to the Army. Each army group and each army had its own Staffel. From 1941 until the end of the war the Junkers 88 was the most used long-range reconnaissance type. This gave excellent service, though on occasions the units operating it suffered heavy losses. This will always be true when individual aircraft penetrate deeply into areas with strong fighter defences.

At the beginning of the Russian campaign the Heinkel 111 was used temporarily by some reconnaissance Staffeln supporting Panzer groups. After the spring of 1942 the provision of long-range air reconnaissance for the Army became a Luftwaffe mission, and that service assumed control of all units. During the period 1942 to 1944 the number of Staffeln assigned to the role, as a monthly average, was twenty-three in 1942, twenty-seven plus in 1943, and twenty-eight plus in 1944. After that came an appreciable fall, to fifteen Staffeln in April 1945.[8]

Towards the end of the war a few Arado 234 twin-jet aircraft operated in the strategic reconnaissance role. This high performance machine flew missions successfully over strongly defended areas such as Great Britain and Western Europe.

Night Reconnaissance Units

On the initiative of the Luftwaffe General with the German Army High Command, three night reconnaissance Staffeln were formed in time for the campaign in Russia. Each Staffel had an establishment of nine Dornier 17Z aircraft equipped for night operations. The strength of this force was more or less constant for the remainder of the war. These aircraft carried parachute flares and flash bombs to permit night photography. The Do 17Z performed satisfactorily in this role, and was replaced later in the war by the higher-performance Dornier 217.

Units Assigned Temporarily to Support the Army
FIGHTER UNITS

The 1935 edition of Air Field Manual No. 16 accepted the possibility that fighters might be placed under Army command. In paragraphs 130 and 131 it stated:

> Fighter and anti-aircraft artillery forces committed in defence missions within operational zones of the Army will usually be under Army command.

At that time the Army's operational zones were considered as areas in which the Army should have unrestricted executive authority over all fields of endeavour. It was thought that the Army should have responsibility for the air defence mission in such areas, and that in turn meant its giving it control over the available forces.

Later experience, from wargames and manoeuvres, led to a recognition that it was not practicable for the Army to have sole responsibility over these areas. Luftwaffe combat units would be stationed [in these areas] with their communications, supply and servicing installations. Some of these areas also contained factories and installations important to the armaments industry but whose defence was not of direct concern of the Army. If the Luftwaffe had to defend these areas it was not feasible to place its forces under Army control.

Moreover, the defence of the battle area could not be handled by fighter and anti-aircraft artillery forces alone. Effective defence was possible only by continuous and destructive bomber attacks on the enemy airfields. Also, when enemy aircraft crossed the Army's operational zone on their way to attack targets outside that zone, defending fighters had to engage them throughout the time they were over friendly territory. In such cases large numbers of fighters would be in the air over an army's zone of operations, only some of which would be engaged in protecting Army installations. To place these fighters under Army control would have led to friction between the Army and the Luftwaffe concerning the operational priorities assigned to the fighter units. In such circumstances uniform direction of air operations would have been impossible.

Another point recognised at an early stage was that the mission of air defence commenced at the aircraft factories and extended throughout the length and breadth of the friendly zone of the interior. It had to be considered as an homogeneous entirety and could not be divided between the Army, the Navy and the Luftwaffe. Air Field Manual No. 16, in paragraph 24, stated correctly that

Attack, defence, and local protection are related missions. They must be directed by a single centre and in accordance with uniform principles.

For this reason a supplement to Air Field Manual No. 16, published before the war, established that fighter forces would be assigned to Army command only

. . . when the situation on the ground made this necessary and the overall situation permitted . . . Luftwaffe fighter units stationed within Army zones of operations or near to such zones for operational purposes, if instructed by the Commander-in-Chief Luftwaffe in agreement with the local Army command, can be employed in operations to prevent enemy air operations over the zone of operations.

This compromise formula was reached only after lengthy discussions with the Army. It confirmed the view that in special circumstances fighter units might be assigned to Army control. In the event, however, during World War II no fighter unit was ever placed under Army command.

As part of its role in supporting the Army, the Luftwaffe was assigned responsibility for the following missions:

1. air defence within the Army zones of operations;
2. action to achieve air superiority over the battle area, above all to safeguard reconnaissance aircraft performing their missions;
3. fighter action in support of combat action on the ground under certain circumstances.

In the light of experience gained in World War I, the Luftwaffe attached great importance to the ability of its fighters to participate in the land battle. When employed in such missions they delivered attacks with guns and bombs, and all fighter types had provision to carry bomb racks under the wings [and/or the fuselage]. Such racks reduced the maximum speed of the aircraft by about 25mph and were fitted only when required.

TACTICAL OR SHORT-RANGE BOMBERS

Until 1938 the Luftwaffe High Command had no front-line units dedicated to provide direct support of the Army. The only such force in existence was part of a tactical trials unit [the Lehrgeschwader]. This experimental unit, equipped with the Henschel 123,[9] was known as the Ground-Attack Gruppe (Schlachtfliegergruppe). With a strength of 40 aircraft, it was organised into three 12-aircraft Staffeln plus a headquarters flight with four aircraft.

At this time it was hoped that static warfare [as in World War I] could be avoided through the use of modern tank forces and air forces. Consequently it was thought that the best way to support Army operations would be through indirect support, by means of air attacks on the rear areas of the combat zone and against the hostile armament industries.

If the occasion arose, Air Force units involved in direct support operations could be committed temporarily in the battle area. However, the controversy did not end there. The decision was postponed until the build-up of the operational air arm was completed and experience had been gained with the experimental ground attack unit. In the Spanish Civil War, an outdated fighter type [the Heinkel 51 biplane] had participated in the land battle with good results. This brought the subject of direct support into the foreground.

Prior to the German occupation of the Sudetenland in 1938, when there was a possibility that an armed conflict might develop, orders were issued for the formation of five so-called ground-attack Gruppen. Two of these received Hs 123s, the other three receiving Ar 68s, He 46s and He 51s. From November 1938 four of the five Gruppen re-equipped with the Junkers 87 and became dive-bomber units. The remaining Gruppe continued as a specific ground-attack unit using the Hs 123. Thus, when war broke out in 1939, there were two types of unit providing direct support of Army operations, the ground-attack unit and the dive-bomber unit.

In the case of the ground-attack unit, this situation remained unchanged during the early years of the war, with only the one experimental Gruppe in existence. Only in 1943 were more ground-attack Gruppen activated, rising to a total of five by September.[10]

During the first four years of the war the dive-bomber units were the main air arm providing direct support of Army operations on the battle area. These also took part in independent air operations, such as attacks on airfields as part of the battle to secure air superiority. The strength of the dive-bomber force varied from an average of about eleven Gruppen in 1940 and 1941 to seven in 1942 and twelve in September 1943.[11]

By October 1943 the dive-bomber units with their outdated aircraft were becoming unsuitable for daylight operations. Consequently the existing dive-bomber Gruppen were reorganised as ground-attack Gruppen and re-equipped with the Focke Wulf 190. This raised the number of ground-attack Gruppen from five to a high point of twenty-four in December 1943. During 1944 the monthly average was twenty-plus Gruppen, falling by April 1945 to seventeen.

SPECIAL AIRCRAFT FOR GROUND ATTACK AND DIVE-BOMBING
In response to invitations from American aero clubs, in 1934 Ernst Udet[12] had travelled to America to participate in air displays. There he made his acquaintance with the Curtiss Helldiver, a shipborne fighter biplane developed by the United States Navy. This aircraft was equipped to carry out dive-bombing attacks on ships and during its display the Helldiver made accurate diving attacks and released its bombs from low altitude.

Greatly impressed by the demonstration, Udet reported what he had seen to the German Ministry for Aviation. The latter provided funds to purchase two of the aircraft and ship them to Germany.

The aircraft Udet brought back prompted the development of improved types of dive-bomber in Germany. This development was not without controversy, however. In his memoirs Ernst Heinkel later wrote:

> American firms, above all Curtiss, had been producing dive-bombers already for several years. There they had given these planes the emotive designation 'Helldiver' because of the extraordinary strains that the dive imposed on the pilot. In 1932 I had produced a dive-bomber, the He 50 for Japan . . . In 1933 and 1934 a few of these planes were constructed for the Luftwaffe, which formed an experimental dive-bomber Staffel.
>
> However, in 1934, when [Wolfram] von Richthofen, later Field Marshal von Richthofen, took over the Development Branch of the Technical Office, the idea of a dive-bomber was nearly killed. Richthofen had stated categorically: 'Diving below 6,600 feet is complete nonsense.' Owing to the state of development of anti-aircraft artillery, he maintained, every plane that descended to such a low altitude would be shot down by anti-aircraft fire . . .
>
> A few of those in von Richthofen's branch . . . did not agree with their chief on this matter, and continued with experiments in this direction. On their own responsibility they carried out tests with the Henschel 123 . . . Nevertheless, Richthofen remained sceptical. It was therefore all the more surprising when, in 1936, a large-scale contract was suddenly awarded for the development of dive-bomber aircraft.[13]

Later, von Richthofen would achieve fame using the very weapon whose development he had opposed. The influence behind the *volte-face* came from Ernst Udet. When this famous aviator succeeded von Richthofen as Chief of the Development Branch, followed in June 1936 by his promotion to Chief of the Technical Office, it came as a considerable surprise. Yet the fateful nature of his appointment, both for the Luftwaffe and for Udet himself, could not be foreseen at the time.[14]

The Henschel 123 was an all-metal biplane suitable for dive-bombing and for ground attack. Five of these planes went into action during the Spanish Civil War in 1937. However, the Hs 123 played no important part in the conflict and it was soon replaced by the Junkers 87 dive-bomber with a better performance.

The prototype Ju 87 appeared in 1935, a highly manoeuvrable all-metal aircraft with a low cantilever wing. A distinctive feature was the inverted gull wing, necessary to keep the legs of the fixed undercarriage as short as possible. It was fitted with dive-brakes to prevent the aircraft gaining speed too rapidly during its attack dive, and the airframe was strengthened to withstand the forces imposed during the pull-out. A later version of the Ju 87 [the Ju 87D], with a more powerful engine and a strengthened undercarriage, could carry a bomb load of up to 4,000lb. One major disadvantage of the dive-bomber was that it could employ its steep diving mode of attack only if the cloud base was above 2,600 feet. When it became evident that the Ju 87 was too slow to survive in combat, these units converted to the ground-attack role and re-equipped with the Focke Wulf 190.

Operational testing of the FW 190 for the ground-attack role commenced early in 1942. This single-seat fighter was powered by an air-cooled engine, which was an advantage because there was no liquid cooling system vulnerable to battle damage. The aircraft was highly manoeuvrable and its battery of cannon and machine guns provided good firepower. The sturdy, wide undercarriage enabled it to operate from field airstrips and the aircraft had excellent take off and landing characteristics.

During the early years of the war dive-bombers were adequate for attacking [lightly armoured] enemy tanks. Following the start of the Russian campaign, however, the tanks being encountered carried thicker armour and were no longer vulnerable to conventional air attack. New ways had to be devised to attack these tanks from the air.

In 1942 engineers at the Experimental Anti-Tank Air Detachment at Rechlin mounted a 37mm cannon under each wing of the Ju 87. The Ju 87, already a slow aircraft, had its speed and manoeuvrability further reduced by these changes. However, against ground targets the pilot could aim these guns with considerable accuracy. Rechlin engineers also mounted a 75mm gun under the fuselage of a Junkers 88. In 1943 the unit, which comprised a Staffel of specially modified Ju 87s and another with Junkers 88s, moved to Bryansk on the Russian Front for operational tests.

The operational tests with the large-calibre gun fitted to the Ju 88 did not continue for long.[15] In contrast, the Ju 87 fitted with two 37mm anti-aircraft type guns produced excellent results. The best results of all were obtained from the twin-engine Henschel 129 carrying a 30mm cannon.[16] In spite of all efforts, however, it was found impossible to assemble sizeable anti-tank air units.

In 1945 it was decided to establish a few provisional Staffeln equipped with recoilless anti-tank weapons [but these did not enter service before the war ended].[17]

Night Ground Attack Operations

Soon after the start of the Russian campaign the Red Air Force began employing light biplanes to carry out night harassing operations over German-held territory. The most-used type was the [Polikarpov] U-2, which carried a light bomb load and penetrated only short distances behind the battle area.[18]

[Appreciating the value of this type of operation,] in the autumn of 1942 the [Luftwaffe] Air Fleets in the East improvised their own night harassing Staffeln using available aircraft types. Shortly afterwards the High Command formally established several night ground attack Staffeln. Initially these units operated obsolete combat types such as the Arado 66, the Heinkel 45 and the Heinkel 46, trainers such as the Gotha 145 and liaison aircraft such as the Fieseler 156.

By the end of 1943 several of these units were consolidated into Night Ground Attack Geschwader 1. By the end of 1944 there were twelve such Geschwader; four were equipped with Ju 87s, one with [captured Italian] Fiat CR 42 [biplanes] and the rest a mix of types as described earlier. In Italy, Air Fleet 2 employed Fiat CR 42s for night harassing operations. At the time of the Allied landings at Anzio-Nettuno in February 1944, that headquarters also began using Ju 87s in this role as they were no longer suitable for operations by day. The Chief of Ground Attack Forces expressed grave doubts about the move, but in the event the Ju 87 achieved good results in the new role.

Twin-Engine Bomber Units Cooperating with the Army

Luftwaffe bomber units were equipped to execute missions in support of the ground forces. Their usefulness was limited, however, because heavy ground fire in the battle area made it impossible for large aircraft to operate at low altitude to seek out appropriate targets. The best targets for these aircraft lay beyond the battle area, as Air Field Manual No. 16 pointed out in paragraph 21:

> When operating in close cooperation with the ground forces . . . bombers will often be unable to find targets against which they can bring to bear their full striking power, even though the destruction of those targets might provide effective support for the Army . . . It is better to commit these air forces against more distant targets, the destruction or neutralisation of which can exercise a decisive influence on the combat operations of the Army . . . Thus action against the sources of the enemy's military potential might also be advisable even during times of close cooperation with the Army.

From the above, it is clear that the bomber force was to be used in direct support of Army operations only for part of the time.

In 1939 the Luftwaffe began the war with 31 twin-engine bomber Gruppen. By September 1940 the total had risen to 45 Gruppen, and it held this strength until the start of the Russian campaign in June 1941. Three more Gruppen were added during the latter part of 1941, and by September 1942 the force had increased to 47 Gruppen. During 1943 the force reached its peak strength with 54-plus Gruppen. In 1944 the strength fell to 41-plus, with a sharp decrease from August. By April 1945 the number of operational bomber Gruppen had shrunk to about seven.[19]

During the first half of the war the Luftwaffe operated three main types of twin-engine bomber:

1. The Dornier 17. At the beginning of the war the Do 17Z was in service with front-line units. It was particularly suitable for low-level attacks, for which reason these aircraft were assigned primarily to units of Air Corps VIII. From 1941 this aircraft was replaced by the Dornier 217 [though this type was unsuitable for close-support operations].

2. The Heinkel 111 was in use at the beginning of the war and, with modifications, it served until the end of the conflict.

3. The Junkers 88 was intended as the standard Luftwaffe bomber type. The crew comprised a pilot, an observer, a radio operator/gunner who manned the upper rear gun, and a flight engineer/gunner responsible for the downward-firing weapons. The crew sat close together, permitting good communication between them. The plane was equipped to carry out horizontal, shallow-dive or steep-dive attacks. Typical range/payload figures for this aircraft were:

   a. Range 900 miles carrying a bomb load of 3,300lb. If a longer runway was available, the aircraft could carry up to 6,800lb of bombs.

   b. Range 1,400 miles carrying a bomb load of 1,100lb. In the overload condition the aircraft could carry up to 3,300lb of bombs.

   c. Range 1,600 miles with a bomb load of 1,100lb.

Of the forty 40 bomber Gruppen in February 1940, twenty-four were equipped with He 111s, twelve with Do 17s and three with Ju 88s (the type had recently entered service), and one was equipped with the Focke Wulf 200 [for maritime armed reconnaissance operations].

Mobility of Air Units

The permanent authorities such as the local air base command, the air base area command and the Area Command Headquarters were responsible for providing messing, billeting and supplies (fuel, munitions etc.) for air units operating from their area. Thus, when a unit arrived at a new airfield, it had everything it needed to commence operations. This 'lodger' system, in which each tactical unit operated independently of any parent unit, made it possible for a unit to move to a new airfield or theatre of operations as fast as it could fly there.

Luftwaffe combat flying units were not tied organically to ground service units. In principle their aircraft could be serviced and maintained by any airfield operating company, anywhere. Each Staffel had a small team of NCOs with specialist knowledge of the airframe, engine, radio systems and weapons of its specific type of aircraft. These men supervised the work carried out by the airfield operating company. The specialist NCOs flew to the new base in one of the operational aircraft, if there was room, or in a transport plane attached to the unit.

Each bomber Gruppe had two airfield operating companies. During a move to a new airfield, one operating company moved there in good time before the rest of the unit. Thus when the aircraft arrived at the new base they could resume operations almost immediately. In contrast to the bomber units, reconnaissance and ground-attack units were dependent on their organic motorised ground service elements. When moving to a new area they took advanced servicing parties with them, so that they were able to resume operations temporarily until their full ground component arrived. Tactical reconnaissance units had adequate motor transport and personnel to enable them to establish and maintain a forward tactical airstrip in addition to their main base airfield.

Munitions for Ground Support Operations[20]
FRAGMENTATION BOMBS

Even before World War II it was understood that the available SD 10 (22lb) and SD 50 (110lb) fragmentation bombs could be effective against closely massed personnel, for example troop assemblies or columns.

In view of the Army's stated requirement for direct support, however, it was expected that there would be attacks on dispersed infantry or similar targets, and against dug-in targets. A new type of weapon, the SD 2 (4.4lb) fragmentation bomb, was developed specifically for use against such targets. These bombs could be dropped in large numbers from low-flying aircraft, the aim being to cover a large area rather than strike at an individual target.

For the start of the Russian campaign selected fighter, dive-bomber, and bomber units were equipped to carry SD 2s. According to a May 1941 report from the Chief of Special Supplies and Procurement Services (Generalluftzeugmeister),[21] eight twin-engine bomber Gruppen (five with Ju 88s and three with Do 17s) were equipped with racks to carry 360 bombs per aircraft. Seven single-engine fighter and dive-bomber Gruppen (four with Messerschmitt 109s and three with Ju 87s) were equipped with smaller racks to carry 96 bombs per aircraft. After the campaign opened it was planned to equip two Gruppen of twin-engine fighters [Me 110s] with racks to carry 96 bombs per aircraft.

While battle fronts remained fluid, the SD 2 proved highly effective, although the expenditure of these bombs often exceeded supply.[22] Once the ground situation became stabilised, however, the Soviet anti-aircraft defences became far more dangerous. Low-altitude attacks, necessary with this type of bomb, could then be carried out on a limited scale and then only by single-engine aircraft. Only in the final stages of the war, in situations of extreme emergency, were these bombs again used in appreciable quantities.

DEVELOPMENT OF CLUSTER MUNITIONS

It soon became evident that the need for SD 2 bombs to be released at low altitude was a serious operational disadvantage. It is astonishing that the Luftwaffe High Command failed to realise the usefulness of very small bombs scattered in very large numbers over targets. Following the campaign in France in 1940, the Luftwaffe captured more than a million 2.2lb [cluster-type] bombs designed to be delivered against targets in large containers. The bombs captured in France could have been used without difficulty. They could have been fitted into the German containers used to carry incendiary bombs, which were available in quantity. However, without consulting the field forces, the Luftwaffe General Staff released the captured bombs for scrap. Copper was scarce in Germany and the idea was to salvage the small quantities of copper in the detonators. Only when it was too late was the value of these bombs realised, and then the weapons had to be produced in Germany.

The SD 1 (2.2lb) fragmentation bomb proved particularly effective following the introduction of a new container, the AB 250, which held 225 of the small bombs. Itself shaped like a bomb, this container had good ballistics and could be aimed accurately. A set time after leaving the aircraft, a detonator fired to open the container and spill out the small bombs. The latter then covered a large area on the ground. Sometimes these small bombs found their way into foxholes or trenches without overhead protection, making them extremely effective as anti-personnel weapons.

In 1943 the present author commanded Air Division 1 operating in the central area of Russia. On one occasion units of the division employed these bombs during an attack on a wooded area where Russian troops had assembled prior to an attack. Afterwards German troops entered the wooded area without encountering resistance and found what could be termed, in the truest sense, a 'dead man's wood'.

Despite efforts by the responsible authorities, it was not always possible to produce these bombs in anything like the numbers required. In February 1943, during a conference on Special Supplies and Procurement Services, Generalfeldmarschall Erhard Milch commented:

At the front there is a badly felt need for 2.2-pound (1 kilogram) bombs ... What are profitable targets for these weapons? In their rear areas the Russians move forward in gigantic columns. They march in columns three abreast with horses, horse-drawn vehicles and vehicles three abreast. The infantry march across terrain, widely dispersed in groups of ten, twenty or forty ... If enough small bombs were available, we could rain these down on them.

Once the snow has melted and the cover is thin, enormous results could be achieved with the 2.2-pound bombs, especially if these missions could be flown by the Luftwaffe more frequently than now. Against massed targets, which are to be found in large numbers and whose destruction would have decisive effect, it is necessary to use the 2.2-pound bomb.

If I can strike these people with small bombs that would be a gigantic achievement. Throughout the summer the Russians will want to do nothing else but attack. Either they will march forward to attack us, or we can attack them and they will march rearwards. In either case I must be there with the small bombs, which will decimate them and break their morale.

Air Fleet 4 and Generaloberst von Richthofen have reported that they have submitted requisitions [for these weapons] but have received nothing. They could deliver the entire production of 350,000 of these bombs on targets in single day. This output is far too small. Another point is that we have none of these bombs stockpiled in depots, so that they cannot be made available at the front.[23]

It was found, however, that the responsible German field commanders often failed to appreciate the effectiveness of these bombs as an anti-personnel weapon.[24]

NEW ANTI-TANK WEAPONS

During the war against Russia, combating the tank became a problem of the first magnitude. The German Army had far too few anti-tank weapons, so the Luftwaffe had do what it could to help in this area. Due to the fault of the German High Command [that is, the failure to build up a strong heavy bomber force], and because many of the Russian tank factories lay beyond the range of German [twin-engine] bombers, [few attacks were made on factories with a view to reducing production]. Instead it was necessary to destroy the tanks, laboriously and one at a time on the battlefield, under heavy fire.

[The fitting of large-calibre cannon to aircraft for anti-tank operations has been described earlier in the chapter]. With the ever-increasing need to provide the means to combat tanks from the air, large-calibre, high-explosive bombs (1,100lb) were used as an emergency measure. The difficulty of hitting dispersed tanks was fully realised, and the large-calibre bomb was chosen because a near miss might put a tank out of action. It was found, however, that the blast from such a bomb would incapacitate a tank only if the detonation was within about 12 feet of the target. Moreover, it was important to detonate the bomb immediately above the ground, without penetrating the surface. If the bomb entered the ground, that channelled the blast upward instead of sideways. In practice it was rare to put a tank out of action with a near miss.

Experience soon showed that the chances of scoring a direct hit on a tank were better using a large number of small-calibre bombs. As a result, a special anti-tank bomb was introduced, the SD 4Hl, weighing 8.8lb.[25] The hollow-charge warhead could pierce armour as thick as five inches, and it achieved good results against tanks. These weapons also had a fragmentation effect, making them useful against infantry operating with the tanks. These bombs were packed in 1,100lb containers, each holding 78 SD 4Hls. The containers were dropped in a steep-dive attack [the effect of the weapon was rather like a shotgun blast aimed at the target]. The chances of achieving a direct hit [with one of the small bombs] were much better than for a 1,100lb bomb. The SD 4Hl was carried mainly by Ju 87s, and when these aircraft were replaced in 1944 its use decreased considerably.

The FW 190s which replaced these aircraft could not make accurate, steep-diving attacks.

BOMBS FOR USE AGAINST PERMANENT FORTIFICATIONS

In 1939 and 1940 the general-purpose bombs in use proved reasonably effective against the obsolete fortifications found in Poland, Belgium and Holland. They were not so effective against modern fortified points such as those of the French Maginot Line or the Russian fortifications around Sevastopol. On this subject General Plocher has written:

> Direct hits, even with the heaviest bombs (3,000 to 5,000 pounds), did not neutralise permanent fortifications. These weapons had a really annihilating effect only in attacks on batteries in open emplacements.[26]

The SH 250 [550lb] hollow-charge bomb was a more effective weapon for use against such fortifications. A January 1942 report by the Chief of Special Supplies and Procurement Services gave the following analysis of its effectiveness:

> Using the hollow-charge principle, against fortified works these bombs achieve a penetration of at least 10 feet in concrete, and of almost twelve inches in armour plating.[27]

This bomb entered service too late for practical use, however, because, following its introduction, fortifications of this type were never attacked.

BOMBS FOR TRAFFIC-INTERDICTION

At the beginning of the war a variety of bomb types were available for use against these targets. The only weak area was in attacks on rail lines, when these bombs would often ricochet off the ground and detonate some distance away without damaging the track. This was particularly likely where the line was on a raised embankment, a favourite point for air attack because a crater there was more difficult to repair than one on flat ground. To prevent such a ricochet, bombs were fitted with a nose spike[28] to hold them in place after impact.

In 1941 the Chief of Special Supplies and Procurement Services arranged an operational trial using different types of bomb against sections of Russian rail track. That October he gave the results of the tests:

> Attacks were carried out on a section of the Orscha–Lepel rail track. The results were as follows:

SC 10 [22lb General-Purpose] Bombs. These weapons are unsuitable because they cause damage to the track only if they detonate very close to the lines.

SC 50 [110lb General-Purpose] Nose-Spiked Bombs. These render Russian rail tracks unusable if they detonate within 5 feet of the rails. The damage can be repaired by filling the bomb crater and replacing the damaged ties and rails, and this can be accomplished in a relatively short time.

SC 250 [550lb General-Purpose] Nose-Spiked Bombs. These bombs inflict more lasting damage to Russian railways than the SC 50 type nose-spiked bomb, if they detonate within 15 feet of the rails.

Spike-nosed bombs should be released in a shallow dive from about 165 feet. Most bombs dropped in this way will lodge in the ground, though a small percentage might still ricochet.[29]

The report stated that from November 1941 about a thousand SC 50, five hundred SC 250 and five hundred SC 500 spike-nosed bombs would be available each month.

Two SC 50s could be carried by the Messerschmitt 109, and four each by the Messerschmitt 110 and the Ju 87. When it was fitted with bomb racks under the fuselage, the Me 110 could carry eight of these bombs. As to the larger SC 250, the Ju 87B or R versions carried one bomb, while the later Ju 87D could carry three. The Me 109 could carry one, the Me 110 and Dornier 217 could carry two, and the Ju 88 could carry four of these weapons. For the SC 500 spike-nosed bomb, the carrying capacity of each plane was the same as for the SC 250.

BOMBS FOR ATTACKING INLAND WATERWAYS

For attacking stationary targets such as canals, bridges, lock gates, ship-lifts and other port installations, warehouses and wharves, normal general-purpose bombs were available. Mines were also laid by aircraft in canals and waterways. Thus in July 1942, for example, the Wehrmacht High Command ordered that the lower reaches of the Volga river should be mined to interrupt traffic by enemy shipping. A few minelaying sorties were also flown to disrupt traffic through the Suez Canal.

BOMBS FOR ATTACKING ROADS

General-purpose bombs were used in attacks on road targets such as embankments or junctions. During mobile operations it was found that enemy troop movements could be hindered by bombs placed at the entrance to or exit from built-up areas, to collapse houses and cover the road with debris. The bombs used were the same as those employed in attacks on cities.

Throughout the war the destruction of man-made structures [i.e. bridges or viaducts] was one of the most effective ways of interdicting road traffic. The same can be said of interdicting rail or waterway traffic. Paragraph 166 of Air Field Manual No. 16 mentioned the advantages of destroying large, important structures 'which take a long time to restore to use'.

Attacks on emergency bridges built by military engineers, and in particular pontoon bridges, were more difficult. In such cases enemy ground defences and smokescreens often made it impossible to achieve success during high-altitude or dive-bombing precision attacks. For example, in March 1945 the Commanding General Air Fleet 6 reported to the Commander-in-Chief Luftwaffe that it was almost impossible for German aircraft to hit the Russian bridges across the Oder river because when aircraft approached the bridges the Russians immediately set off smokescreens to conceal them. The Air Fleet therefore suggested using the Wasserballon (water balloon) floating mine or other special weapons against the bridges.[30] As early as February 1945 the Commander-in-Chief Luftwaffe had authorised the release of two hundred spherical floating mines from Army stocks to Air Fleet 6, for use against bridges. Only one mission was flown with this type of mine, by [Heinkel 111s of] 7th Staffel Bomber Geschwader 4. No information is available on the results they achieved. To counter the German use of drift mines, the enemy erected nets upstream of the bridges to protect them.

Due to the critical battle situation it was decided to dispatch Mistel composite aircraft to attack the bridges on the night of 14–15 April 1945.[31] These achieved no noticeable results either.

Training of Luftwaffe Personnel for Army Support
OFFICER TRAINING

The older generation of officers assigned to the higher command positions of the Luftwaffe had, in almost all cases, been members of the Army. Some of these had attended the Army Staff College and received training as Army General Staff Corps officers.

During their training the younger generation of officers received instruction in the basic concepts of army tactics. In the Air Command and General Staff School (Luftkriegsakademie) established at Gatow in 1935, participants received instruction on army tactics and attended map manoeuvres.

A few General Staff Corps and other officers participated in a one-year course to train them for joint military command posts. Later this training took place at a Joint Command and General Staff School (Wehrmachtakademie). During this course, joint military operations were covered as a special study. In addition, the Army and the Luftwaffe exchanged senior officers to serve as participants or observers, during the annual manoeuvres conducted separately by the two services.

TRAINING OF FLIGHT PERSONNEL

After their basic flight training, flight personnel went to the Air Weapons Schools (Fliegerwaffenschulen) for theoretical and practical training in tactics. There was instruction on army support operations, and the participants flew missions involving reconnaissance and the use of weapons against simulated targets of all types. The Luftwaffe maintained separate schools for training crews for reconnaissance aircraft, fighters, dive-bombers and horizontal bombers.

Early in 1938 the Army initiated a system under which commissioned and selected noncommissioned officers were detached to the Luftwaffe to receive flight training as observers serving with tactical reconnaissance units.

TRAINING AIR UNITS IN ARMY SUPPORT

This subject received comprehensive treatment in tactical air reconnaissance units attached to the Army (Aufklaerungsfliegerverbaender-Heer). As part of this training, from 1936 these units were allocated to appropriate Army commands (divisions, corps, etc.) to which they would be assigned in time of war. These Army commands were authorised to include their allocated air reconnaissance units in all manoeuvres. Also, as a matter of principle, officers on the Army command staffs and the air reconnaissance units took part in each other's field exercises and map exercises.

During the initial stages of the Luftwaffe build-up, the subject of providing direct support for Army forces was neglected. Nevertheless, air units participated in Army manoeuvres and this undoubtedly benefited training and cooperation between them. During field exercises the Army was also authorised to request the Luftwaffe to fly practice missions to allow ground troops to practise active and passive air defence measures.

Sizeable Luftwaffe forces participated in Army manoeuvres, and particularly during the 1937 joint service manoeuvres.

Despite these moves, Luftwaffe command circles took the view that air support for the Army should take the form of indirect support through attacks on targets in the enemy rear rather than direct support in the battle area. As late as the spring of 1939, the plans provided for dive-bomber units to operate against targets in enemy rear areas.

These views changed only as a result of experience gained in the Spanish Civil War. Early in 1939 the prospect of a large-scale war became a clear possibility. General von Richthofen, the last officer commanding the Condor Legion in Spain, assumed command of Air Corps VIII which included several dive-bomber units. Following this move, there was a period of intensive training for these and other Luftwaffe units that worked closely with the Army.

In 1937 the Army detached a Tactics Instruction Staff (Lehrstab fuer Heerestaktik) for assignment to the Inspectorate for Air Reconnaissance and Air Photography. The aim was to promote an understanding of Army tactics in the Luftwaffe, and in particular of mobile operations by armoured and motorised infantry divisions. Also, in demonstrations by the Lehrgeschwader, command personnel kept abreast of the latest ideas regarding the employment of air forces in support of the Army.

REGULATIONS GOVERNING
COOPERATION BETWEEN THE ARMY AND THE LUFTWAFFE

The basic ideas governing cooperation between Luftwaffe and Army forces were set down in Air Field Manual No. 16. A separate field manual entitled 'Operations' (Truppenfuehrung) formulated the tactical principles for Luftwaffe units assigned under Army commands in the time of war. In addition, several publications were produced for issue to intermediate and high-level command personnel.

In February 1939 a Tactical Experience Unit (Gruppe Taktische Erfahrungen) was established as part of the Operations Division of the Luftwaffe High Command. This unit prepared bulletins and other material on tactical matters, and ensured their proper distribution.

WEAKNESSES IN THE LUFTWAFFE TRAINING PROGRAMME

Despite the measures outlined above, training in the Luftwaffe was inadequate at the start of World War II.[32] During the expansion in the late

1930s the Luftwaffe formed many new units in a very short time. In 1938 Hitler issued a directive calling for the Luftwaffe to make a five-fold expansion in strength by the end of 1942. As part of this expansion, in 1939 the Luftwaffe split most flying units into two, thereby doubling the number of units. The requirement to train the necessary extra personnel placed firm limits on the rate at which the expansion could proceed. Shortages of raw materials and manufacturing capacity led to delays in producing the necessary aircraft and equipment. As a result, during the short time between then and the outbreak of the war, all units could not be brought to full strength. The reorganisation took up so much time and effort that tactical requirements received relatively little attention. Thus, when the Luftwaffe entered the war, it was far smaller than provided for in the long-term expansion programme. Numerically, its strength was sufficient to fight only a single-front war.

During the early stages of the war, because of the overwhelming superiority of the German military forces compared with their enemies, these weaknesses were not apparent. War itself was regarded as the best training school. There can be no doubt that the establishment of specialised courses then would have proved profitable later in the war, when combat became more severe. By 1942 Germany was committed to a multi-front war and the Luftwaffe was unable to meet its many responsibilities. The High Command took the short-sighted view that the enemy's numerical superiority made it impossible to spare personnel for proper [post-graduate] training courses. Once America, Britain and the USSR fielded their modernised and greatly expanded air forces, the Luftwaffe was in a hopeless situation.

Notes to Chapter 2

1. As mentioned elsewhere, the Luftwaffe controlled a large part of the anti-aircraft artillery force.
2. The Heinkel 45 was a single-engine, two-seat biplane with a maximum speed of 180mph. The Heinkel 46 was a single-engine, two-seat, high-wing monoplane with a maximum speed of 155mph.—A.P.
3. The Henschel 126 was a single-engine, two-seat, high-wing monoplane with a maximum speed of 221mph.—A.P.
4. In fairness it should be pointed out that during the early part of World War II tactical reconnaissance was neglected by every nation, and all air arms operated obsolete or low-performance aircraft in this role. Yet during each of the land campaigns during this period the Luftwaffe rapidly secured air superiority, allowing its obsolescent

tactical reconnaissance aircraft to operate without interference from enemy fighters. Their counterparts in opposing air forces were not so fortunate.—A.P.

5. The Focke Wulf 189 was a twin-engine, three-seat monoplane with an extensively glazed crew compartment giving excellent all-round visibility. Maximum speed was 217mph.—A.P.

6. Although experimental helicopters were certainly flying in Germany at that time, their development was at an early stage. It is therefore unlikely that these machines could have operated effectively in the harsh conditions encountered at the battle fronts.—A.P.

7. When he wrote this section the author was obviously unaware of the developments in the RAF and the USAAF, which were using fighter types modified to carry out aerial photography and other reconnaissance tasks. Flown by pilots trained in artillery reconnaissance and spotting, these aircraft carried out such missions on a regular basis. For photography at low altitude, the aircraft carried a fixed oblique camera and performed the task effectively even when the targets were in well-defended areas. The author was correct in saying that aerial survey work and night and bad-weather reconnaissance could be carried out effectively only by multi-seaters; but these tasks represented only a small part of the total reconnaissance effort.—A.P.

8. Statistics showing monthly figures are available in the original manuscript and also in the translated draft of USAF Historical Study No. 163, Karlsruhe Document Collection.

9. The Henschel 123 was a single-engine biplane with a maximum speed of 212mph.—A.P.

10. Technical data in unpublished appendices, USAF Historical Study No. 163, Karlsruhe Document Collection.

11. Ibid.

12. Ernst Udet was the top-scoring German fighter pilot to survive World War I.

13. Ernst Heinkel, *Stuermisches Leben* (Stormy Life) (Stuttgart, 1953), pp. 331–3. English edition ed. by Jurgen Thorwald (New York, 1956).

14. In October 1941 Ernst Udet held the rank of Generaloberst and was in charge of the development and production of aircraft for the Luftwaffe. Following the heavy losses in German aircraft suffered on the Eastern Front, his production programmes were failing to produce enough planes to replace these losses. Also, several of the new combat aircraft which should then have been on the point of entering service had run into difficulties. Udet was driven to such a state of despair that he committed suicide.—A.P.

15. Almost all the cannon-armed Ju 88s were shot down within a short time of commencing operations. The Junkers 87D, fitted with 37mm cannon and redesignated Ju 87G, was more successful and this version remained in operational service in small numbers until the end of the war.—A.P.

16. The twin-engine Henschel 129 armoured ground attack aircraft carried a built-in armament of two 20mm cannon and two 7.92mm machine guns. The aircraft had provision to carry a 30mm high-velocity cannon with a 30-round magazine in a bulge under the fuselage, making it the first armoured assault aircraft to carry a heavy

cannon. The aircraft failed to realise the hopes placed in it, however, because its engines proved unreliable under combat conditions. The ingress of dust into the cylinders via the carburettor intakes caused excessive wear, and engine failures were common. As a result, the serviceability of the Hs 129 was poor and there were never more than about fifty of these aircraft available for operations.—A.P.

17. The weapon was the 77mm SG 113 Foerstersonde, four of which were mounted vertically in streamlined fairings fitted in the wings of the FW 190. These weapons were triggered by a magnetic sensing system, as the aircraft flew low over the tank it was attacking. To balance the recoil forces from the armour-piercing shells fired downwards, counterweights were fired upwards from the opposite end of the barrels. The weapon performed successfully in tests early in 1945, but so far as is known it was never used in action.—A.P.

18. The Polikarpov U-2 general-purpose, two-seat biplane carried a bomb load of up to 440lb when employed in night harassing operations. This type of operation involved little diversion of effort, but it caused considerable disruption to road traffic in enemy rear areas at night. Vehicles showing lights were liable to come under attack without warning. If they drove with their lights out, there were large numbers of traffic accidents.—A.P.

19. Statistics showing monthly figures are available in the original manuscript and the translated draft of USAF Historical Study No. 163, Karlsruhe Document Collection.

20. Details of bomb types used in Army support missions are in Appendix No. 39 in unpublished appendices, USAF Historical Study No. 163, Karlsruhe Document Collection.

21. Letter, Generalluftzeugmeister (Chief of Special Supplies and Procurement Services), Document No. 3800/41. Karlsruhe Document Collection, F V 1aa.

22. These small cylindrical weapons had a diameter of 3in and a length of $3^1/2$ in. Originally they were carried in special containers that fitted on the bomb racks of the attacking aircraft. Once clear of the container, the casing of the SD 2 opened to form 'wings' and it spun to the ground like a sycamore seed. The opening of the 'wings' caused the weapon to decelerate rapidly and the aircraft should have been well clear of the fragments thrown up when the bomb detonated. During a normal attack run that was so, but from time to time an SD 2 'hung up' inside its container without the crew realising it. If the jolt of landing freed the weapon, it fell away and detonated on striking the ground. Several German aircraft were destroyed or damaged in this way, and this led to the SD 2 being withdrawn from service for a time.

23. Generalluftzeugmeisterbespreghung (Chief of Special Supplies and Procurement Services Conference), Karlsruhe Document Collection, F V 1aa.

24. The SD 2 bomb (see note 22) was also used in large numbers as a cluster munition.

25. 'Hl' was an abbreviation for Hohlladung, meaning 'hollow-charge'.

26. 'Die deutsche Luftwaffe an der Ostfront' (The German Air Force on the Eastern Front), Vol. 4, 122, Karlsruhe Document Collection.

27. Report, Generalluftzeugmeister (Chief of Special Supplies and Procurement Services), Document No 18/42, 8 January 1942, Karlsruhe Document Collection, C VI 2.

28. Called the Dinort rod after its inventor, Major Oskar Dinort, who later commanded Dive-Bomber Geschwader 2. At the end of the war he held the rank of Generalmajor.

29. Letter, Generalluftzeugmeister (Chief of Special Supplies and Procurement Services) to Commander-in-Chief Luftwaffe, 29 October 1941, Karlsruhe Document Collection, F V 1aa.

30. A document on the development of Wasserballon is included in a report from Air Force 6, dated 26 February 1945, Karlsruhe Document Collection, C VI 2.

31. From the War Diary of the Luftwaffe High Command, 1945, Karlsruhe Document Collection, C VI 2.

The Mistel comprised a Junkers 88 bomber with a Messerschmitt 109 or FW 190 fighter mounted rigidly on struts above it. The crew compartment of the bomber had been removed and replaced with an 8,400lb, shaped-charge warhead. The flying control surfaces of the two aircraft were linked electrically (the first ever fly-by-wire system), so that the pilot of the fighter could fly the combination to the target. Once within a few miles of his objective he aligned the combination on the target in a 15-degree descent. At a distance of about 3,000 yards from the target he engaged the bomber's autopilot, then fired explosive bolts fitted to the supporting struts to release the fighter. The explosive-laden Ju 88 maintained its heading and (it was hoped) impacted the target and detonated.

Lacking an effective heavy bomber able to carry super-heavy bombs, the Mistel was the only means the Luftwaffe had to deliver a really large warhead against an important target. The limitations of the weapon are obvious, however. Given the relatively low speed of the Ju 88 during its final run, about 300mph, the weapon was affected by crosswinds and it was less accurate than a normal bomb. The Ju 88 was also vulnerable to ground fire.

The Mistel was originally intended for use against large targets such as capital ships or dams. It was unsuitable for attacking relatively small targets like bridges, but by 1945 the military situation had deteriorated to a point where weapons that had even a small chance of success had to be used in the desperate attempts to halt the Soviet advance.—A.P.

32. It should be pointed out that in this respect the Luftwaffe was better off than most, possibly all, of the air forces that opposed it during the early part of the war.—A.P.

Part Two

Army Support Operations

CHAPTER 3

Aerial Reconnaissance Operations[1]

Types of Operations

The purpose of aerial reconnaissance was to furnish information on the approach of enemy forces, forward or rearward moves by enemy forces and the current location of enemy reserves. There was particular emphasis on mobile units, the construction of defensive fortifications and changes and developments in the enemy rear areas. It was important to carry out frequent cover of rail and road routes in the enemy far rear, and over the areas with open flanks. The army commands would base their operational decisions on the information thus obtained.

The purpose of tactical air reconnaissance was to provide information for the command and operation of troops in the battle area. This included information on the dispositions of enemy forces and the construction of enemy defensive positions. An important item was the identification of motor and armoured vehicles in the battle area.

Once the opposing ground forces were in contact, the tactical mission developed into battlefield reconnaissance and artillery reconnaissance. With other intelligence data available to the army command, battlefield air reconnaissance was to furnish information to assist in the conduct of land action. Information was required on the positions of enemy forces, the disposition of artillery and the location of reserves and armoured units. It was also important to know of any other developments behind the battle front. Battlefield reconnaissance units were also to report on the locations of the forward friendly infantry and armoured units, and their progress during the ground battle.

Air units employed in artillery reconnaissance had two primary missions. First they furnished target data for friendly artillery to engage enemy artillery moving into new firing positions; and secondly they were to correct the fire from friendly batteries and report the effects of that fire.

Paragraph 85 of Air Field Manual No. 16 defined the division of aerial reconnaissance areas, between those units allocated to the Army and those under Luftwaffe command:

Generally the areas in which the Luftwaffe will conduct aerial reconnaissance
will be farther in the enemy rear than the aerial reconnaissance areas of the Army
and the Navy. Whenever possible, these areas will be delineated by a line marked
by a series of distinct geographical features.

This assumed that the Luftwaffe would be employed primarily in the
conduct of operations far behind the battle area. Throughout World War
II, however, air power was employed in direct support of the Army to a far
greater extent than anticipated. As a result, targets for air attack (including
enemy airfields) were usually located within the Army air reconnaissance
areas.

Sometimes the Army and the Luftwaffe conducted reconnaissance in
the same areas. Units operating with the Army were frequently tasked with
observing enemy lines of communication, such as rail or road routes.
Often this involved flying in a nearly straight line to the limit of the
aircraft's radius of action. Units carrying out missions for the Luftwaffe,
in contrast, flew zig-zag tracks as they moved from one target to the next.
In practice, therefore, the reconnaissance missions differed in their
execution but not in their operating areas. It was impossible to avoid some
duplication, though often this resulted in a more detailed picture. In any
event, special organisational and communications measures (covered later
in this section) ensured a constant interchange of information between the
Army and the Luftwaffe.

The Army High Command established the boundaries for air reconnaissance zones allocated to the various army groups. These in turn
determined the zones of cover for the units attached to the various field
armies. Deviations from this rule sometimes became necessary when the
long-range units available were inadequate for the task. This was the case,
for example, along the Western Front during the Polish campaign in
September 1939. During this period Army Group C, with three armies
responsible for defence of the West Wall, had only three Staffeln available.
Consequently the entire front was divided among these three units, with
no regard for the operational boundaries of the individual field armies. In
Russia also, because of the large areas and the inadequate number of long-
range reconnaissance aircraft, it was necessary to divide the front into
arbitrary zones without regard for the frontages of individual field armies.

During the 1939 campaign in Poland and the 1940 campaign in the
West, the Army High Command held two long-range Staffeln in reserve.
These uncommitted units were used to secure additional cover during

unclear or decisive situations. The situation at Kutno[2] in the Polish campaign, and the assignment of long-range air reconnaissance units to keep under observation the evacuation of British troops from Dunkirk, were examples of such situations.

Planning Aerial Reconnaissance Missions

At army headquarters responsible for directing air reconnaissance, it was essential for officers to have a clear understanding of its capabilities and limitations. After pointing out the speed and comprehensive nature of this 'under favourable conditions,' Air Field Manual No. 16 outlined its limitations. It stressed that air reconnaissance could not reveal details that were not discernible to the human eye or to the camera. Furthermore, its effectiveness was subject to limitations from enemy action, the weather and the time of day. However, the manual concluded, these limitations were at least partially offset by the enormous coverage that it made possible.

Based on World War I experience, these definitions underwent little change during World War II. Army command headquarters were sufficiently acquainted with the subject to realise that aerial reconnaissance could not detect a well-hidden enemy, for example troops concealed in a densely forested area. Also, even using parachute flares and night photographic equipment, it was extremely difficult to locate enemy troop movements at night. Moreover, negative reports provided no grounds for assuming that there were no enemy troops in an area that had been searched by aircraft.

In contrast, it was difficult for non-aviators to realise the extent to which weather hindered reconnaissance operations. At the start of the war tactical air reconnaissance was seriously restricted because aircraft employed in this role lacked blind-flying and radio navigation equipment. Thus the performance of the tactical units contrasted painfully with that of the long-range units. It was difficult for Army officers to appreciate that, while the weather often paralysed operations by the former, long-range machines taking off in the same conditions could fly great distances through cloud and then descend to observe enemy movements in the rear areas.

Air reconnaissance was only one of several sources of information on the enemy. Only when its results were collated with the other information could the new observations confirm [or refute] the information already available.

The appropriate army command had to decide whether a mission was to be a one-off, or one of a series of missions. If the former, it was necessary to decide the timing (for example, a sortie at daybreak to detect the tail-end of a movement during the night). Often it was possible to make the decision only after receipt of the report from the day's first mission. This was the case, for example, if the first reports detected a motorised enemy unit on the move and it was necessary to keep track of it.

The above points governed the direction of long-range and tactical air reconnaissance, and in particular missions over the battlefield. The closer an enemy force came to the front line and the faster it moved, the greater the need to keep it under continuous observation. This applied particularly to armoured or motorised infantry units.

As the campaign in Russia wore on, the Soviet fighters became increasingly effective and these were superior in performance to the German reconnaissance aircraft. To overcome this problem several tactical units re-equipped with single-seat fighter types, and there was also an increase in the use of night aerial reconnaissance.

Because of these changes, the initial German technique of providing continuous observation over the whole of the battle area had to give way to what was called point reconnaissance. Under this system units concentrated their activities in areas of importance, to answer specific questions set by the army commands.

Long-Range Air Reconnaissance

During the campaigns in Poland, France and the Balkans, ten strategic air reconnaissance Staffeln were available. This number was adequate. Before the start of the Russian campaign, on his own initiative the Luftwaffe General with the Commander-in-Chief Army formed a few night reconnaissance Staffeln. Each of these units comprised nine Dornier 17 twin-engine aircraft fully equipped for blind flying and navigation. The intention was to provide one such Staffel for each field army committed in the East. The Commander-in-Chief Luftwaffe approved the formation of only three of these units, one for each of the three army groups in the Eastern Theatre. Each army group headquarters had a command staff which processed requests for missions. With the few aircraft available it was impossible to conduct systematic and continuous reconnaissance at night. Only missions of particular importance, and for which there was a clear prospect of success, were to be flown.

The Heinkel 46 tactical reconnaissance aircraft went into production in 1933 and was obsolete by 1939. During the campaign in Poland many reconnaissance units operated the type, however.

The all-metal Henschel 126 was the main tactical reconnaissance type used during the campaigns in the West in 1940 and the Balkans in 1941. via Schliephake

The twin-boom Focke Wulf 189 tactical reconnaissance aircraft saw extensive use on the Eastern Front and performed well until the strength of the Soviet fighter force rendered such operations by day too costly. From 1943 the aircraft was relegated to the night reconnaissance role.

Dornier 17Fs and Ps of Long Range Reconnaissance Gruppe 121, seen in 1939. Until the end of the campaign in France in 1940 the performance of the Do 17 was adequate for the missions it had to fly.

The Junkers 88D was the mainstay of the Luftwaffe long-range reconnaissance arm on the Eastern Front. Note the three camera ports under the fuselage, and the two 198 Imp. gallon drop tanks under the wings for an extended-range mission. via Schliephake

The Henschel 123 equipped the sole ground-attack Gruppe to go into action with the Luftwaffe during the first two years of the war. via Schliephake

(Above and below) Low-level ground attack has always been a dangerous business. This Dornier 17Z of Bomber Geschwader 76 suffered severe blast damage when, during a strafing run on a French column in May 1940, one of its 20mm cannon shells detonated an ammunition truck.

As well as the losses from normal enemy action, on the Eastern Front Luftwaffe crews had to face the risk of being rammed. This Heinkel 111 of Bomber Gruppe 126 limped back to base after it was struck by a Soviet fighter. Note the propeller slashes along the top of the fin and the damage to the rear of the starboard engine nacelle.

When it entered service in 1942 great things were expected from the Henschel 129 armoured ground-attack aircraft. During operations from forward airfields in Russia its radial engines proved vulnerable to dust ingestion, however. The serviceability the aircraft was poor and it was unreliable in service. Schmidt

The SD 2 anti-personnel bomb weighed 4.4lb. On the Eastern Front the weapon was used in large numbers against soft-skinned battlefield targets and proved very effective. Later in the war it was used as a cluster munition, fitted in a range of containers, the largest of which held 248 of the small bombs.

A line of SD 2s bursting across an airfield in Russia, during an attack by a Junkers 88 of Bomber Geschwader 51. via Dierich

Junkers 87Ds of Dive Bomber Geschwader 5 on their way to attack a target on the Northern Front in Russia. Each aircraft carries a 550lb bomb under the fuselage, and two ABB 250 small bomb containers under the wings. Schmidt

The largest bomb type in general use by the Luftwaffe on the Eastern Font was the 2¹/₂-ton 'Max', here about to be loaded on to a Heinkel 111.

Luftwaffe personnel examining the 30.5cm gun turret at the 'Maxim Gorki' battery at Sevastopol, knocked out by two direct hits from a Junkers 87. via Schliephake

The Heinkel 111 was the main heavy bomber type used on the Eastern Front for most of the war. These examples belonged to Bomber Geschwader 100.

A photograph taken from a German multi-engine bomber making a low-level strafing attack on a column in Russia. During such attacks the Luftwaffe suffered heavy cumulative losses in aircraft.

A Focke Wulf 190F ground-attack aircraft taxies out for a sortie. It carries a 550lb bomb under the fuselage.

Late in the war a few Hs 129B-3s went into action in the anti-tank role carrying a 75mm high-velocity cannon under the fuselage. Slowed further by the draggy gun blister, these aircraft were able to achieve little in the face of Soviet air superiority. via Schliephake

An FW 190 fitted with the 77mm SG 113 Foerstersonde anti-tank weapon. Two of these guns were mounted vertically in a streamlined fairing fitted to each wing. A magnetic sensing system ripple-fired the four barrels in quick succession as the aircraft passed low over the tank. To balance the recoil forces from the armour-piercing shells fired downwards, counterweights were fired upwards from the top of the barrels. Early in 1945 the weapon performed successfully during tests, but so far as is known it was never used in action.

Thus, at the start of the Russian campaign the Army had thirteen strategic reconnaissance Staffeln. These were too few to cover the huge expanse of the Eastern Theatre. It was not even possible to assign a Staffel to each of the highest level commands in the East (three army groups, seven armies and four Panzer group headquarters, plus the headquarters of Commander-in-Chief Army). Since the tactical units had only a limited night capability, the night reconnaissance Staffeln had to provide both long-range and tactical night air reconnaissance in their assigned areas. Beforehand it was thought that Luftwaffe aircraft conducting their own missions would supplement the intelligence secured by the Army's reconnaissance units. To an extent this was so, but from the outset the Army's missions failed to produce as clear a picture as during the earlier campaigns.

At the start of the campaign [in Russia] Army Group South was responsible for a frontage of 420 miles, extending from the Black Sea in the south to the Pripyat Marshes in the north. With only four strategic air reconnaissance Staffeln to serve the headquarters, three armies and one Panzer group, it had to conduct its operations in a manner different from that in previous campaigns. One Staffel was assigned to the Eleventh Army, on the right flank operating separately from the rest of the front. Two Staffeln plus a night Staffel operated under the army group headquarters, covering the area ahead of the Sixth and Seventeenth Armies. The remaining Staffel was assigned to First Panzer Group.

An important factor governing the aerial reconnaissance operations was the radius of action of the aircraft available. During the campaigns in Poland and in the West the factors restricting the depth to cover were the geographical and political borders of the nations involved. In the Eastern Theatre the restricting factor was the range of the available aircraft. The Junkers 88 was the best strategic air reconnaissance type the Luftwaffe had available. Yet, while its radius of action was adequate for the field army headquarters, it was inadequate to meet the requirements of the Luftwaffe High Command, the Army High Command and the army group headquarters. Had there been an aircraft available with a longer operating range, it could have detected the transfer of enemy divisions from Siberia to western Russia by keeping watch on the rail routes though the Ural mountains. [In the winter of 1941 the unexpected arrival of reinforcements from Siberia halted the German advance into Moscow. These reinforcements then launched a counter-offensive that threatened to force German troops into retreat.]

Another factor to be considered when planning missions was the strength and behaviour of the enemy air force. During long-range missions flown by individual aircraft, this was less important than for tactical and battlefield reconnaissance missions. During the campaign in Russia the author saw no evidence of attempts at systematic fighter operations to counter [German] strategic air reconnaissance.

Requests for long-range air reconnaissance came from the appropriate army command headquarters, usually in writing. Frequently the mission assignment contained instructions for several days ahead, and included a supplement with detailed orders. These instructions covered the following points:

1. Supplementary information on the enemy that was important for the execution of the mission.
2. Information on enemy fighter or anti-aircraft defences.
3. Information on the commitment of friendly bomber or fighter forces [in areas through which the reconnaissance aircraft was flying].
4. Details on the depth and width of the areas to be covered for long-range and perhaps tactical reconnaissance.
5. The requirements of the specific mission, with emphasis on the information needed by the army command. This usually included details on road and rail routes and other targets, such as defence installations, to be photographed.
6. Required reporting method. This might stipulate, for example, that if the crew saw signs that enemy troops had crossed a specific river or terrain feature they were to report this by radio.
7. Instructions for tactical air reconnaissance to be carried out when passing over areas of interest, if applicable.

As an example of an actual mission assignment, these were the instructions from the Fourteenth Army, part of the Southern Army Group, for aerial reconnaissance on the first day of the Polish campaign, 1 September 1939 [the aircraft involved was a Dornier 17]:

1. *Areas to be Reconnoitred*
   Northern boundary line for Fourteenth Army aerial reconnaissance operations: Beuthen–Miechow–Sandomierz.
   Depth to which reconnaissance is required: To a line from Sanok–Zhyrow–San to Przemysl–Sandomierz–Lublin.

Line of division between operational (army) and tactical (corps) air reconnaissance.

Air reconnaissance: Popradtal to Neusandez–Limanowa–Mussyna–Grybow–Bochnia–Krakow–Wolbrom–Pilica [river].

2. *Instructions to 4th (Long-Range) Staffel Reconnaissance Gruppe 14 on long-range air reconnaissance for Fourteenth Army Headquarters*

Observe enemy troop movements in front of the Fourteenth Army, traffic on rail and road bridges over the San and Dunajec rivers and defensive preparations at these rivers.

Observe activities of troops in and near Krakow and at the troop training grounds at Bojanow (15 miles south-east of Sandomierz). For this purpose the following must be kept under observation:

a. *Rail routes:* Premysl–Chyrow–Sanok–Jaslo–Neusandez; Przemysl–Jaroslav–Rzeszow–Tarnow–Krakau; Rzeszow–Jaslo; Tarnow–Neusandez.

b. *Road routes:* Przemysl–Sanok–Krosno–Jaslo–Gorlice–Neusandez; Jaroslav–Rzeszow–Debica–Tarnow–Krakow; Sandomierz–Debica–Jaslo; Tarnow–Neusandez.

The strategic Staffel is to detect the presence of and movements by sizeable enemy forces in and from the following zones:

a. From Krakow along the main highways to south and west as far as Nyalenice–Wadowice–Trzebinia.

b. Any unloading taking place on the rail route between Tarnow and Krakow.

c. The Sanok–Krosno area (between one and two enemy divisions). It is particularly important to detect any movement south, towards Slovakia, from the last-named area.

Concurrent missions for the strategic Staffel:

a. Keep under observation the road route Gdow–Mylenice–Wadowice–Andrychow (field fortifications).

b. Detect whether there is a bridge over the Vistula river at Baranow (12 miles south-west of Sandomierz). (Air photos required.)

3. *Tactical Air Reconnaissance for Army Corps*

Army Headquarters attaches particular importance to the early recognition of areas where stiff enemy resistance might be encountered. It requires information on the status of field fortifications and troop concentrations (permanent fortifications in the Polish industrial region of Nikolai–Pless–Bielitz–Saybusch).[3]

Instructions like those above were customary when the various army command headquarters had tactical control over units. The tactical air support command staffs assisted in drawing up these instructions. After the Luftwaffe assumed responsibility for tactical air reconnaissance for the Army, the procedure changed. Luftwaffe liaison teams at the various army headquarters served in an advisory capacity, and forwarded requests for missions to the appropriate Luftwaffe commands. These commands coordinated the army requirements with their own reconnaissance plans and forwarded them, as orders, to the units.

Tactical, Battlefield, and Artillery Air Reconnaissance

In planning tactical reconnaissance missions it was essential to use material obtained from long-range missions, if this could be done without causing undue delay. If no results were available from long-range reconnaissance, tactical units had to operate farther afield.

So long as tactical Staffeln remained under the control of the Army, orders for tactical, battlefield and artillery reconnaissance went from the army corps or armoured division headquarters to their assigned Staffeln. By the start of Russian campaign a Gruppe command staff, together with a tactical Staffel, were assigned to each Panzer corps. Also an armoured division tactical air reconnaissance Staffel (Aufklaerungsstaffel Panzer) was assigned to each armoured division.

During the campaigns against Poland, France and [initially] Russia there were usually sufficient tactical Staffeln available to assign one to each army corps. Only a few army corps had no tactical unit of their own. The latter had to rely on reconnaissance by [aircraft from] adjacent corps and this caused delays in the assignment of missions. Before the Russian campaign additional tactical air reconnaissance Staffeln were activated. This brought the Army's total to thirty-six normal tactical Staffeln, plus twenty armoured division air reconnaissance Staffeln (compared with only thirty tactical Staffeln available at the start of the war).

Compared with those available in the 1939 and 1940 campaigns, however, the tactical reconnaissance Staffeln available for the Russian campaign were weaker. Instead of the nine planes, each normal Staffel had only seven planes. Those Staffeln assigned to the armoured divisions had only six planes each. Moreover, each Staffel no longer held [an operational] reserve of three planes.

In view of the increased frontages held by the individual corps in Russia, and their smaller authorised strengths, the demands made on the Staffeln had to be reduced. To make matters worse, inadequacies in equipment restricted the range of operations. Reference has already been made to the limited capabilities of these aircraft [Hs 126s] during periods of bad weather or at night. This [situation] lasted until the FW 189 became available in quantity.

The factors listed above, and the wide range of mission requirements, imposed restrictions on the control of tactical air reconnaissance units. When the corps and armoured divisions had tactical control over their tactical Staffeln, the mission was formulated in a Special Instructions Annex to the operational order. This contained items similar to those listed previously for a long-range air reconnaissance mission.

For artillery air reconnaissance, the Annex contained detailed instructions for that mission. Thus an observation plane might be needed by the artillery commander of 2nd Division from daybreak on, to report on the fall of artillery fire. A second plane might be required to direct the adjustment of fire from heavy batteries of the corps artillery. These instructions included details on voice radio communication [frequencies and call-signs] and designated points for air-dropping messages.

Such written orders usually applied only to the first missions on a particular day. If further details were necessary, the air liaison officer received the instructions orally and relayed them to the Staffel or, in urgent cases, passed them directly to the crew of the aircraft.

For Staffeln assigned to armoured divisions, instructions were usually given orally. Generally these operations were in the nature of an extended battlefield reconnaissance, which had to keep pace with the frequent changes of plan that characterised operations by armoured units. For this reason instructions were in a brief, concise form. The Staffeln assigned to armoured divisions had highly flexible ground organisations, with specially selected personnel. Communications were primarily by radio.

The responsible army command gave instructions to the Staffel commander, who allocated the missions to crews and issued orders on their execution. Only in exceptional circumstances would the army command pass orders directly to an aircraft crew.

After the Luftwaffe assumed responsibility for Army air reconnaissance [early in 1942], it consolidated the Staffeln into tactical Gruppen. The assignment of missions followed the previously established pattern, however. Where there was no agreed system of cooperation between an army corps and a tactical Gruppe, the corps forwarded requests through its air [liaison] officer. The latter then relayed these to the appropriate air corps or air division headquarters.

Execution of Aerial Reconnaissance Missions

The depth of penetration of long-range missions in the Eastern Theatre was limited by the operational radius of the aircraft. Almost invariably long-range air reconnaissance missions were flown by single aircraft, which flew as unobtrusively as they could and avoided combat if possible. Air Field Manual No. 16, paragraph 91, stated that unit-sized missions might be flown 'against strongly defended areas or targets' requiring heavy defensive firepower. In practice this never happened during strategic missions flown for the Army. Similarly, there is no record of strategic missions having fighter escorts.

Daylight strategic air reconnaissance missions were usually flown at altitudes between 16,000 and 27,000 feet to avoid enemy fighters. Once the aircraft was well behind the front line, it usually descended so that the crew could get a better view of ground detail. Low-altitude missions produced particularly good results, though these had to cease when the Russian fighter defences became more effective.

At night the main purpose of long-range reconnaissance was to detect troop movements on roads, and aircraft flew at lower levels than during the day. They used parachute flares to illuminate the area for observation, and took photographs using flash bombs.

Air photography was used to confirm visual observations, and also during operations at high altitude where ground detail could not be seen by eye. Aerial photographs were required of such targets as rail depots, built-up areas, supply depots and airfields. [Strips of overlapping] photographs of sections of the rail and road networks allowed interpreters to determine the amount of traffic being carried. Immediately the films had been developed, the preliminary interpretation took place [using the negatives].[4] Important films were passed to the proper quarters, with final interpretation being made from prints.

During long-range missions, crews passed reports in flight by radio only in exceptional cases. Such reports could be intercepted by the enemy, they revealed the whereabouts of the aircraft and they increased the risk of fighter attack. The only time radio reports were required in flight was when the army command urgently needed the information. That was the case if, for example, a large enemy motorised force had been detected on the move.

Normally the observer made his oral report on the mission to the Staffel commander after landing. The latter then passed information of particular importance to the appropriate tactical air support command staff or the army command; or he might instruct the observer to report his findings orally to the tactical air support command staff or army command. Usually the oral reports were followed up with a written report on the mission, sometimes with sketches of the targets, forwarded to the appropriate headquarters.

[In most campaigns the] army commands paid full tribute to the work of the strategic air reconnaissance arm. The exceptions were in the Southern and Western Theatres from 1943 on, where the Luftwaffe was markedly inferior to the air forces of the Western Allies. There, aerial reconnaissance operations [by the Luftwaffe] became so difficult that often they failed to detect sizeable movements by enemy forces.

The War Diary of Army Group A covering the 1940 campaign in the West contains many entries on the road and rail movements by French and British Army elements observed by aerial reconnaissance. This information served as the basis for interpreting the current situation. For example, the entry for 25 May stated:

> The available intelligence information was supplemented during the afternoon by air reconnaissance, which reported enemy forces moving north and north-west (towards Ostende and Dunkirk) from the Lille–Dounai–Valenciennes area. This weakened the [previous] assumption that these forces intended to act in concert with those south of the Somme, and emphasised the need to complete the envelopment in the north.

As in the case of those engaged on long-range missions, aircraft flying tactical, battlefield and artillery reconnaissance missions flew singly and tried to avoid air combat. When the enemy air force was particularly active, it was customary to fly a fighter sweep through the area to coincide with the reconnaissance operation. In practice the arrangements for a coordinated action of this type were usually agreed between the reconnaissance and fighter units concerned. This was particularly the case when the units used the same airfield or airfields close to each other. Thus cooperation was always excellent between the tactical Staffeln and Fighter Geschwader Moelders [No. 51] in Russia. Moelders fulfilled every possible request from the reconnaissance units. Elsewhere, however, the tactical units usually had to fly their missions without fighter protection.

When the strength of the Russian fighter force increased to the point where tactical air reconnaissance became difficult, some units re-equipped with single-seat fighters fitted with cameras. These planes always operated in pairs, one pilot carrying out the reconnaissance while the other watched for enemy fighters. Occasionally, in areas where Russian fighters were very active, it was necessary to commit the planes in formations of four.

Of course, these fighter-type aircraft could not carry out all types of reconnaissance missions. Their primary task was to keep road routes under observation, a mission they could execute flying at low altitude. The altitudes at which daylight tactical missions were flown varied according to the type of reconnaissance required, the weather and the enemy defences. Tactical missions extended to a depth of 120 miles behind the main enemy line of resistance. Usually the aircraft crossed the front line at high altitude then, once over the enemy rear, if required it descended to lower altitudes the better to detect ground detail. Fighter-reconnaissance aircraft were well suited to such operations because of their good speed and climbing performance and their manoeuvrability. When engaged solely on photo-graphic missions these aircraft flew at high altitude, 16,000 feet or above, as the weather allowed [for example, medium-level cloud might force them to conduct their photography from lower levels].

Daylight battlefield reconnaissance missions were usually flown at altitudes around 6,600 feet, or much lower if the mission required the detection of ground detail or the observation of advancing friendly troops. [The success of] battlefield air reconnaissance depended largely on the air situation. In many cases planes assigned such missions had to be protected by fighters or anti-aircraft artillery. During night operations aircraft had to operate at very low altitude.

Usually artillery observation planes had to adjust their operating altitude to the requirements of their particular mission. For example, a plane observing fire from heavy guns firing on a flat trajectory against targets far in the enemy rear flew as high as clear observation allowed. A plane assigned to observe fire from smaller-calibre guns, or report the general accuracy of artillery fire, flew at low altitude back and forth between the target and the friendly artillery positions. Otherwise these aircraft behaved in much the same way as battlefield reconnaissance planes, and they, too, sometimes required protection from fighters or anti-aircraft artillery.

Often the army commands employed tactical units to produce photographic map surveys of large areas. For example, they might require continuous-strip photos of specific areas such as rivers or defensive fortifications. In Russia, where maps were incomplete and contained inaccuracies, the photos were used to prepare photographic maps, true-to-scale air photographic mosaics and normal maps. An example of this was the mapping work done as part of the preparation for the crossing of the Dnieper river in 1941. The assigned reconnaissance Staffel flew along the road, taking photographs with an approximate scale of 1:20,000 that plainly revealed the detail along the shores of the river. As a result it was possible to prepare quickly a gridded photographic map in four sections to the same scale as the photographs. This map, printed in two colours, was issued to command staffs and the assault boat and engineer detachments.[5]

Following the introduction of the FW 189 into service, with a night operating capability, the use of night reconnaissance increased. One factor forcing this shift was the increasing strength of the Russian fighter force. From January 1943 the 4th (Tactical) Staffel Reconnaissance Gruppe 31, for example, flew night missions on both sides of the Smolensk–Lirssno highway to a depth of 60 miles. Another example of a successful night mission by the same unit was the effective direction of artillery fire at night against the Veliki Luki rail depot.[6]

Sometimes inadequate night air reconnaissance had adverse repercussions on the conduct of operations. An example was during the Polish attack on the German Eighth Army on 10 September 1939, when the Poles achieved tactical surprise with superior forces. The Polish General Kutzreba considered that the Germans had underestimated the strength of the Polish force (three infantry divisions, two brigades and one regiment of cavalry) because their aircraft flew reconnaissance missions only by day. As far as possible the Polish forces confined their movements to the hours of darkness, since, as General Kutzreba observed, 'We had already learnt from experience that the German air forces . . . usually ceased operations before evening.'

The lesson from the above incident is that dusk air reconnaissance had been neglected. In World War I great importance had been attached to missions flown at dusk. These often detected the start of troop movements, while missions flown at dawn often detected the tail-end of such movements. Later in the war, early-morning and late-evening aerial reconnaissance flights became common practice.

It was a serious omission that the High Command failed to attach greater importance to night missions before the war, and develop appropriate aircraft and institute special training. Air Field Manual No. 16 merely stated that at times night aerial reconnaissance 'might be necessary'.

Reporting Aids and Techniques

[During air reconnaissance missions observers carried] point maps (Punktkarten). These had precisely surveyed features such as road intersections, bridges and large and distinctive buildings (for example churches or factories) marked by a black dot and a number. An observer reported his observations and/or targets using the point number and stating the latitudinal and longitudinal distance of the object from that number. Such maps could be produced speedily using field type equipment. Frequent use was also made of grid maps. In this method a map or an aerial photograph was divided into squares, and any targets observed were reported accordingly. Small celluloid overlays were used to determine subdivisions of squares.

Tactical and battlefield reconnaissance planes, particularly the latter, passed reports while airborne by voice radio to their Staffel headquarters. The air liaison officer attached to the appropriate army command would listen in to these reports. Artillery observation planes also reported by voice radio while airborne, speaking directly to the artillery unit they were supporting. If radio communication failed or if the ground unit had no air–ground radio, messages were air-dropped. In the latter case a smoke cartridge was released with the message to facilitate its location on the ground. In special cases, for example to give the precise location of an enemy artillery position, the observer might remove the film from the camera and air-drop it to an army unit with facilities to develop and interpret it.

Usually the aircraft's observer reported on the mission orally to his squadron leader or air liaison officer, immediately after landing at his base. Important items from the report were relayed immediately to the appropriate headquarters. In special cases the observer might deliver his report in person to the appropriate headquarters.

As in the case of reports on long-range missions, discussed previously, the items in the observer's oral report were amplified in a follow-up written report which gave the following:

1. Assigned mission.
2. Track and altitude of flight.

3. Types of maps used.
4. Precise details, usually in chronological sequence, on the observations, with precise information on the location and time of each.
5. Unconfirmed observations or assumptions, stated specifically as such.
6. Details on air photos taken.
7. Description of the air situation: enemy aircraft sighted, with details on the types, time and altitude of observation, information on the air combat if applicable, and whether anti-aircraft fire was encountered.
8. Miscellaneous items: weather conditions, technical failures in flight, etc.

Processing and Interpreting Aerial Photographs

To assure the speedy interpretation and intelligent use of the many aerial photographs by the ground forces, it was essential to have a special air photographic service organisation. Generally the air photographic section of the unit whose planes had taken the photos developed the films and made the preliminary interpretation from the negatives. The purpose was to discover whether the photographs revealed anything that required immediate action. The first step was to decide whether the information should be passed immediately to the appropriate army headquarters, or whether a repeat mission was required.

If the area photographed was within the battle zone, the film was forwarded without delay to the photographic section of the field army headquarters concerned. This section received intelligence data from other sources (for example, agents, the interrogation of prisoners, ground reconnaissance etc.) and could use the photos to confirm other intelligence data or use the latter to facilitate interpretation of the photos. The results were then passed as rapidly as possible to the commands in the form of photographic interpretation reports.

The results of the aerial photographic interpretation were reported in various ways. Simple results were given in written air photographic interpretation reports. Aerial photographic overlays were used to assist in reporting the more complex findings.

Exchange and Dissemination of Results

The speedy and adequate dissemination of information obtained from aerial reconnaissance required close attention and special measures. Like the army commands, the Luftwaffe also had an interest in the results. It might be required it to commit forces against targets found in this way, as part of its army support mission.

For the above reasons, aerial reconnaissance reports were constantly being passed between the tactical air support command staffs and liaison teams attached to army group, army and Panzer group headquarters, and between the various Army and Luftwaffe commands. Usually this exchange of information was handled by the G2 sections, but in particularly important cases it was handled by the G3 sections, the Chiefs of Staff or even commanding officers.

In spite of all these careful arrangements, it was natural that some friction developed in this interchange of information. Prior to the Russian campaign, the Commander-in-Chief Luftwaffe issued detailed orders on the interchange of intelligence from aerial reconnaissance. Reports were to be consolidated at air fleet and air corps headquarters, and the headquarters of the close support air commands under them. Intelligence sections at these headquarters were responsible for the examination of all intelligence reports, and for an appropriate selection to be disseminated. They also decided which headquarters and staffs should receive which reports, and by what means they should be distributed.

Three times each day, the tactical air support command staffs issued a digest of information from reconnaissance reports which was broadcast by radio. So far as they were of general interest, reports from air units other than those engaged in reconnaissance were included in these broadcasts.

The orders stressed the need to make proper use of information obtained from photographs, and to pass on the information thus received. Special attention was drawn to the need to maintain secure communications channels. In addition, the orders contained instructions for the exchange of liaison officers between the tactical air support units and the tactical air support staffs attached to the *Panzer* groups, air corps, armies, army groups and air fleet headquarters.[7]

Return to Luftwaffe Control
of Units Formerly Allocated to the Army, 1942

The immense size of the Eastern Theatre placed excessive demands on the available [Luftwaffe] forces. As a result, the organisational system in use [early in the campaign] was no longer effective and drastic changes were necessary to economise in the use of forces. Due to the need to conduct operations in a number of theatres [i.e., not only that in the East], the Luftwaffe General attached to the Commander-in-Chief Army and his tactical air command staffs could no longer exert effective direction over air units. In addition to the tactical air support staffs attached to the various army commands, the Luftwaffe commands cooperating with these army commands also assigned liaison officers to them. This irrational system of dual representation caused a lot of friction.

By the late autumn of 1941 the operational capability of the aerial reconnaissance units allocated to the Army had diminished seriously. They had suffered heavy attrition of equipment, particularly in aircraft and motor vehicles. At the same time they had received inadequate replacements and supplies, and were often short of fuel. By the end of the year the operational strength of the Staffeln had fallen to an average of between one and two aircraft each. The expenditure of effort in maintaining ground services for the individual Staffeln was no longer commensurate with the number of aircraft they operated. Of the fifty-six tactical Staffeln committed at the start of the Russian campaign, only nineteen were still in action at the end of 1941. The other thirty-seven had to be withdrawn. The strategic Staffeln suffered similar problems.

Since the Commander-in-Chief Luftwaffe could not maintain these units at full strength, the only alternative was to amalgamate the air reconnaissance units attached to the Army with those of the Luftwaffe. Through a strict rationalisation of resources it was possible to maintain a limited number of units in action. In February 1942 the revised channel of command provided for the Luftwaffe to assume responsibility for providing aerial reconnaissance for the Army. At the end of a transitional period, which lasted until the winter of 1942, no Luftwaffe flying units were to remain under Army tactical control. Instead, Luftwaffe reconnaissance units were to cooperate with the army command headquarters in the same way as other air units. Long-range air reconnaissance for army command headquarters became an additional mission for Luftwaffe strategic units.

The possibility of transferring the responsibility for army air reconnaissance to the Luftwaffe had been broached by the Wehrmacht High Command after the 1940 campaign in the West but was opposed by the Commander-in-Chief Army. The Army was unwilling to become more dependent on the Luftwaffe than it was already. Moreover, the Army contended, not without cause, that long-range missions in support of air operations were often conducted in a manner incompatible with Army requirements. Because of this, the Army and the Luftwaffe had conducted their aerial reconnaissance separately during the early part of the campaign in Russia.

The mission of tactical and battlefield reconnaissance for the Army (including that for the artillery and the infantry) was assigned to the tactical Gruppen formed by amalgamating the former Army Staffeln. The number of Gruppen was kept as small as possible, and only thirty-five were formed. These Gruppen came under the control of the various air corps or air divisions, which designated Staffeln to operate with specific infantry corps or armoured divisions. In addition to providing air reconnaissance for the Army, these Gruppen also assumed responsibility for flying tactical missions for air corps and air divisions. Some Staffeln re-equipped with single-seat [fighter type] aircraft fitted with cameras, but the majority continued to operate the FW 189.

The Chief of Aerial Reconnaissance Forces remained with the Commander-in-Chief Army during the transitional period, serving in an advisory capacity and providing liaison with the Commander-in-Chief Luftwaffe. Operating under the Chief of the Luftwaffe General Staff, he had no tactical or disciplinary authority over units but served as inspector of aerial reconnaissance units, training schools and replacement units.

After the transfer of Army air reconnaissance to the Luftwaffe, the latter assumed responsibility for passing the intelligence thus gained to the various army commands, via the air liaison sections and air liaison officers. The advantages of the new system over the old were as follows:

1. It avoided the duplication of effort (particularly long-range missions) which resulted when Luftwaffe-controlled and Army-controlled reconnaissance planes operated over the same areas.
2. The clear-cut chain of command [was an improvement over] the previous divided command authority, under which the Army exercised tactical command over units and the Luftwaffe exercised disciplinary and administrative control.
3. A more flexible use of air power was possible than had been the case when the units were controlled by the Army.
4. The establishment of the aerial reconnaissance Gruppen and the assignment of these to higher-level air commands, whose headquarters were usually located nearer to the units than the controlling army headquarters had been, facilitated supervision.

5. The integration of the [Staffeln] with their parent [Gruppen] ensured a better flow of replacements as regards aircraft, equipment and fuel.
6. The amalgamation of Staffeln under Gruppen headquarters reduced the size of their ground service organisations. With one airfield being required for a Gruppe, its Staffeln made more economical use of the available servicing personnel and equipment.

On the other hand, some there were also some serious disadvantages that resulted from the new system:

1. The reduction in tactical air reconnaissance units made it impossible to assign one Staffel to support each infantry corps or armoured division. Instead, a single Staffel had often to fly missions for several army headquarters.
2. A Staffel supporting an army command could no longer fly from an airfield near the army command it was supporting. Instead it had to operate from the Gruppe air base, which was usually farther away. This, and the factor described in 1 above, loosened the previously close contact between a Staffel and the army headquarters it was supporting. In many cases this complicated the assignment of missions and the process of reporting.

For the above reasons the new system could be considered only as an interim solution. In the case of long-range reconnaissance, it did not lead to any real saving in forces. The Army required long-range aircraft to observe road and rail routes, enemy rear areas and lines of communication extending as far back as the plane's operating radius allowed. Thus [as mentioned earlier] they usually flew in a nearly straight line to the limit of their radius of action. Aircraft engaged in reconnaissance for the Luftwaffe, on the other hand, flew zig-zag tracks from one assigned point target to the next. Because of this, it was usually still necessary to employ two separate aircraft to fly the two types of reconnaissance.

It would have been better, at the start of the Russian campaign, to give tactical air support command staffs the status of a tactical air command headquarters. They should then have had command authority over all tactical air forces, including aerial reconnaissance units, engaged permanently in supporting the Army. Like the strategic air reconnaissance forces, the tactical air reconnaissance units provided reliable support for the Army during World War II. Wherever they were committed, they earned the appreciation of Army commanders and troops.

Notes to Chapter 3

1. This chapter is taken largely from General der Flieger a. D. Karl Drum, 'Der Einsatz dem Heer Taktisch unterstellten Verbaende der Luftwaffe' (Operations of the Luftwaffe Army Support Units), Karlsruhe Document Collection, F III 1a.

2. Kutno, an important rail centre, was a key point in the decisive Battle of the Bzura in which a Polish army was captured on 15 September 1939.

3. Dr. Elze, 'Der Koluft 14 im Polnischen Feldzug, 1939' (The 14th Air Support Command in the Polish Campaign, 1939), Karlsruhe Document Collection.

4. Called the 'wet interpretation' (Nassauswertung) because often the negatives were still wet.

5. Dr. Theodor Stocke, 'Die kartographische Vorbereitung des Dnepr Uebergangs 1941 beim LII Korps' (The Cartographic Preparation for the Crossing of the Dnieper in 1941 by the LII Corps), *Wehrwissenschaftliche Rundschau*, Vol. VI (1956), pp. 202–3.

6. Report to General der Flieger Karl Drum by Oberst Nagel, wartime commander 4th Staffel, Air Reconnaissance Gruppe 31.

7. 'Richtlinien für das Gewinnen von Luftaufklaerungsmeldungen durch die Verbaende des Ob.d.L. und des Ob.d.H., ihren Austausch, und ihre Verwertung fur die Zwecker der Luftwaffe und des Heeres' (Directives for the Processing of Air Reconnaissance Reports through the Units of the Luftwaffe High Command and the Army High Command, their Exchange and their Utilization for the Objectives of the Luftwaffe and the Army), Luftwaffe High Command, Operations Staff Ia/II, 20 April 1941, Karlsruhe Document Collection.

CHAPTER 4

Combat Air Operations

Air Defence of the Army

The air defence of the Army was not a separate mission [for the Luftwaffe]. Normally this formed part of its primary mission to secure air supremacy, or at least temporary air superiority, over the battle area. As early as 1935 Air Field Manual No. 16, in paragraph 103, described the achievement of air superiority as the air force's primary mission:

> Combat action against air forces must be taken from the very beginning of war. Neutralisation of the enemy air force weakens the enemy's military power and serves to protect friendly military forces, the civilian population and the nation. It also releases offensive air units for the execution of other missions of vital military importance.

General Hans Jeschonnek, Chief of the Luftwaffe General Staff, emphasised that defeating the enemy air force was the principal objective of the Luftwaffe. Therefore, the forces participating in the initial attacks had to be as strong as possible. He said that during the first few days of a war the mission of providing air support for the Army was less important than the counter-air mission: 'The damage inflicted on a hostile army in the first two days of a war is in no way proportionate to the damage an enemy air force might inflict if it can operate freely.'[1]

Hitler, speaking shortly after the Allied invasion of Normandy in 1944, stressed the vital importance of securing air superiority. He said it was more decisive than any other single factor in warfare and gave almost complete freedom of movement, while the lack of it led to immobility.

Before the start of each new campaign it was necessary to examine whether the Luftwaffe commitment was to be strong enough. Did it have a large enough margin of superiority [over the enemy air force] to allow army support missions to begin immediately the campaign began? Or should all available forces, initially, partake in the operations against the enemy air force?

Once the Allies had built up their air forces, it became impossible for the Luftwaffe to establish air supremacy. From then on the Luftwaffe had to restrict its efforts to establishing temporary local air superiority over zones of army operations. When this was no longer possible in combat against the Western Allies, first in Italy and later in France, German ground operations inevitably failed.

To protect army units from air attack, the available fighters were shared among the major army formations. Usually a fighter Geschwader with three or four Gruppen operated within the command zone of each army group. It came under the command of the air fleet or air corps headquarters responsible for air operations in that zone. During friendly or enemy offensives, or if the air situation became critical, these forces sometimes received temporarily assigned reinforcements. After 1943, however, this was usually only possible at the expense of other sectors of the front.

[In the spring of 1944 the strength of the Luftwaffe fighter force on the Eastern Front] was quite inadequate, considering the strength of the Russian Air Force and the length of the battle front. The home air defence situation [i.e., the large-scale Allied bombing attacks on targets in Germany] made it impossible to allocate reinforcements to the Eastern Theatre. Another factor that impaired [the effectiveness of] fighter units in the East was that combat action there was regarded as part of the pilots' training. Once they had gained combat experience in that theatre, the majority of fighter pilots were transferred to home defence units. Their replacements were newly trained fighter pilots with no combat experience.

Luftwaffe tactical principles of air defence usually required fighters to go into action from a scramble take-off, when the approach of an attacking enemy force was reported. For this purpose part of each unit was held at cockpit readiness (Sitzbereitschaft), prepared for immediate action. The rest of the unit was at normal alert. Usually rest periods were granted only at night or during bad weather.

German tactical doctrine rejected the notion of standing patrols by fighters over or in front of the battle area [as a matter of course]. Only during offensive operations would the armoured units spearheading a drive receive near-continuous fighter protection. The same fighter units also provided escorts for German bombers.

One problem which defied practical solution was that of providing an adequate defence against the Russian ground-attack units. To attack army forward positions these aircraft ran in at low attitude in formations of between three and eight aircraft, and then returned immediately to Russian territory. Even after a scramble take-off the German fighters usually reached the area too late to effect an interception. Because the Russian planes approached at very low level, they often failed to appear on radar. Pursuing these aircraft over Russian territory was usually a fruitless endeavour, because they flew too low for normal air combat and their protective armour made them difficult to shoot down. Moreover, German fighters trying to attack them came under intense defensive fire from the ground. The only realistic solution was for the troops to protect themselves using their own weapons, or to take cover. Usually, the damage done by these Russian air attacks was insignificant.

Despite the deficiencies outlined above, the German fighter force on the Eastern Front acquitted itself well in its mission to protect ground forces from air attack. This was possible mainly because of the superior quality of German flying personnel and the German aircraft. The best evidence [for German air superiority] was to be found in the scale of rail and road traffic observed behind the Russian and German front lines, respectively. Except during major offensives, roads and rail routes behind the Russian lines were usually devoid of traffic during the day. On the German side, in contrast, road and rail traffic proceeded almost without hindrance. Of course it was different in other theatres of operations, where the German fighter defences were overwhelmed by the numerically superior enemy air forces. [It was also different on the Russian Front during the Soviet summer offensive in 1944, when the weak German fighter force was overwhelmed.]

Types and Scope of Air Support

It is in the nature of air power that attacks on large, compact targets are far more profitable than those against small targets in the battle area. The latter [vehicles or troop positions] were usually widely separated and sometimes dug in to protect them from artillery fire. Even during mobile operations vehicles moving near the front were usually well dispersed and their crews exploited any available cover.

Another factor to be considered was that the enemy concentrated the bulk of his weapons in areas near the battle front, and many of those weapons could be used against aircraft. This became important when German aircraft needed to operate at low level to attack small targets. As a result, our aircraft incurred heavy losses in terms of both those shot down and those rendered inoperable by battle damage.

In a tank battle, even if it was possible to destroy all the enemy tanks, one large Russian tank factory could have made good the losses with a single day's production.[2] An attack that destroyed a tank factory, or put it out of operation for a time, reduced the output of tanks by many times more than could be destroyed individually in the battle area.

On this subject, Air Field Manual No. 16 stated, in paragraph 120:

> Within the scope of the general conduct of the war, combat action by air forces will generally provide indirect support for the combat operations of the other military services.

Obviously, the effects of such indirect support took longer to become evident, but when they did they could have decisive importance. Operations against enemy ground forces produced more rapid results, but their effects were more localised.

Considering the direct cooperation between the Luftwaffe and the Army during important operations, we can observe the manner in which it was accomplished. There are two ways to perform the direct support or cooperation mission, namely:

1. air action against enemy transportation and communications targets, to isolate the battle area; and
2. air action against targets in the area closer to the front line, described as tactical or close air support operations.

Usually German Air Force units supporting the Army employed both methods, performed simultaneously but in separate locations.

This combination of methods to support the Army was applied with great success during the Polish campaign and during the 1940 campaign in France. This method formed an integral part of the Blitzkrieg during the early years of the war and played a decisive role in later phases of the conflict.

Owing to their manoeuvrability, the single-engine dive-bomber and ground-attack aircraft were the only types that could be committed in air support missions in the battle area without risk of heavy losses. Yet the radius of action of these types was inadequate to permit their use over the enemy rear areas. Conversely, the twin-engine bombers [that could reach the enemy rear areas] were unsuitable for close support operations in the battle area. Thus enemy elements that passed through the interdiction belt unscathed were again threatened by air attack when they reached the battle area.

Although the two forms of direct army support were usually applied in combination, they were subject to separate principles and the operations took place in separate areas. So [in this account] it is appropriate to examine them separately.

Interdiction of the Battlefield

The German High Command realised that during large-scale army operations, air action to prevent enemy forces reaching the front was an effective way to influence the battle. Large-scale ground operations required the movement of huge numbers of personnel and vast quantities of matériel. These had to move [to the battle area from centres] far to the rear. Usually the interdiction of these movements had an impact on the land battle within a few days. Air attacks on these targets [troops and vehicles concentrated on roads] produced more profitable results than attacks on the well-dispersed targets in the battle area.

For the most part, German air attacks on communications targets in rear areas aimed to weaken the enemy and create favourable conditions for ground operations. Nevertheless, the objectives of such an action varied according to the military situation. Early in the war or during mobile operations, it was possible to use the Luftwaffe to prevent enemy forces reaching a certain area or phase line within a given time. This allowed German troops to advance into an area and occupy it before the enemy arrived. Before or at the beginning of an important offensive, the Luftwaffe might attack communications and weaken the enemy so that German operations would proceed successfully. On the other hand, if the enemy was preparing to launch an offensive, the Luftwaffe might be asked to prevent the offensive or weaken it to such an extent that German forces could repel it.

Another task was to influence the strength ratios [in the battle area] in favour of the German side, either temporarily or permanently. On the Eastern Front this became almost a permanent mission for the Luftwaffe, because of the relative weakness of the German ground forces. Often the intention was to gain time to allow German ground forces to move into an area in strength, or prevent the enemy from bringing to bear his overwhelming numerical superiority. On other occasions the Luftwaffe tried to prevent the departure of enemy forces from specified areas. This might arise when the enemy tried to move troops and supplies to establish a defensive line ahead of the German advance.

Air Field Manual No. 16, in paragraphs 162–177, established the principles regarding air operations to interdict enemy troop movements.[3]

Troops and supplies moved forward by the following means: by cross-country marches on foot; by truck along roads; by rail; and in certain circumstances by ships [or barges] on inland waterways or rivers. The mission of the Air Force was to destroy the means of transportation or otherwise disrupt these movements.

To achieve such a programme of interdiction, Air Field Manual No. 16 laid down the principal categories of targets:

1. all types of moving columns and march movements;
2. troop concentrations;
3. rail interdiction targets (including rolling stock and permanent installations);
4. road interdiction targets;
5. waterway interdiction targets;
6. man-made structures [bridges, viaducts, etc.];
7. port installations.

Because of the large number of targets, careful selection was necessary. Thus the Manual laid down that it was essential to pick the targets of the greatest importance.

To assure success in operations to seal off the battlefield, precise information was needed on the scope and capability of the enemy transportation system. These conditions were different in almost every country with which Germany came into conflict.

Information on permanent installations in the transport and communications networks had to be collected during peacetime. Such data appeared in the relevant volume of 'Military-Geographical Description' (Militaer-geographische Beschreibungen), issued on several countries. Some of these went into great detail, with tables listing the structures and giving their location, construction and vulnerability to attack.[4] Another valuable source of information was the rail and road route maps issued by the Army Transportation Division. These showed all rail and road routes in a country and gave their carrying capacities.

After the outbreak of war the available data were updated continuously using information from air reconnaissance, agents' reports and the interrogation of prisoners. The data changed frequently owing to developments in the military situation. Thus, for example, the delivery of 427,284 American trucks to Russia[5] caused a pronounced change in the working of the Russian transport system.

With this data, and a knowledge of the military plans, it was often possible to plan air operations to interdict the enemy transport system before the war started. Thus the 'Instruction for the Strategic Assembly and the Conduct of Combat Operations' (Aufmarsch- und Kampf-anweisung), a Luftwaffe contingency plan, included a section on how to interdict enemy communications. Issued for the first time in 1936, these instructions applied if there was a war against an adjacent country. To conceal their purpose, from 1938 they appeared as Tactical Problem White, Red, etc. (Planstudie Weiss, Rot, etc.), with a separate colour to denote each country. The Transportation Division of the Army General Staff, the best-informed source on possible enemy transport systems, assisted in preparing plans to interdict transport routes.

Plans for the interdiction of the transport system were not restricted to rail routes but included roads that might be important during military operations. This was in case a potential enemy used the roads, or shifted to road transport after important rail routes had been destroyed. Thus plans were prepared during peace for the destruction of important roads in time of war. Before the campaign in France, for example, the operational directives of Air Fleet 2 listed the best targets for interdiction attacks to prevent movement by road.[6] Throughout the war similar traffic interdiction plans were prepared and put into effect.

The decision to seal off a battle area was taken by the Wehrmacht High Command, and might follow a request from the Army High Command. If the area to be sealed off did not exceed the zone of operations of an army group, the decision was usually taken at the air fleet/army group or air corps/army level. This presupposed that the air and army commands concerned had received the appropriate instructions from the Wehrmacht High Command.

The mission was executed by the Luftwaffe headquarters responsible for the control of the forces in the area concerned. Usually this was an air corps or air division or, in exceptional circumstances, a local air command headquarters. Before the army commander finalised a request, he usually conferred with the officer directing the air operation or with [air] liaison personnel. This was the only way to ensure that the capabilities [and limitations] of the air units available were considered. According to paragraph 125 of Air Field Manual No. 16, the ground commander should restrict himself to 'stating the purpose to be achieved by the Luftwaffe operations'. The Luftwaffe officer controlling the flying forces then decided how best to execute the mission. In the rare event of a divergence of opinion between the two services, the decision was taken by the next superior headquarters.

This arrangement ensured that Luftwaffe officers with appropriate training handled the execution of air combat missions, and did so according to the proper operational and tactical principles. The Luftwaffe commander was responsible for observing the principle established in Air Field Manual No. 16 that 'too frequent changes in the objective, which would prevent the operation having maximum effect, will not take place'.

When the mission assignment had been completed it might address the requirements in the following manner:

1. The purpose of the action is to prevent enemy columns crossing a line extending from A through B and C and farther west; or
2. The purpose of the action is to interdict rail routes from A to B, C to D and E to F, if possible to prevent movement for four to five days.

For operations to seal off a battle area the responsible air command had available its assigned bomber forces. Also, during the initial phase of the war, dive-bomber units might be available if their operating range was adequate for the task. Dive-bombers were particularly valuable for attacking point targets. Fighter units escorted the bomber and dive-bomber forces, both of which were vulnerable to attack from enemy fighters. After executing their escort mission, or if the Luftwaffe had air superiority in the area, the fighters attacked ground targets.

The execution of attacks on moving enemy columns and transport routes did not differ widely from the methods employed in attacking other similar targets. Usually the attacking units operated at intermediate altitudes. If the air situation allowed, units might also deliver low-altitude attacks. Indeed, as Air Manual No. 16 observed, the effect of low-level attacks on the morale of the enemy troops 'will often exceed the physical damage done'. Usually, the manual continued, [twin-engine] bombers were unsuitable for low-level attacks. When the battle reached its climax, however, it might be advisable to throw in all available units to tip the balance. To keep losses within reasonable limits, the Manual advised that whenever possible it was important to exploit the element of surprise.

In 1941 the Luftwaffe was highly successful in driving the Russian Air Force from the battle area. [Having thus achieved air supremacy,] it created the conditions under which flights of two or three bombers could fly armed reconnaissance missions. These small units were very manoeuvrable and their operations were more flexible than those of larger units. Also, they could attack targets that would not have been worth attacking with larger units. For example, planes on armed reconnaissance could attack trains on the move or lying stationary in dense forests; or, on early-morning missions, they might find the tail-end of a night troop movement and attack it. Later, when the air situation became more difficult, such armed reconnaissance missions could be flown only by fighter-bombers.

A factor that complicated interdiction attacks was that the targets were usually very narrow but also long [i.e., a road, a rail line or a major bridge or viaduct]. Rail tracks were particularly narrow targets. When attacking these the aircraft approached the track at an acute angle and dropped its bombs at short intervals in a stick. This gave a good chance of at least one direct hit on the permanent way, or a bomb landing close enough to it to inflict damage. When attacking with nose-spiked bombs, planes had to release these weapons from low altitude. Because of this, aircraft often attacked rail tracks in areas where there was little risk from defensive ground fire.

Except for the armed reconnaissance missions, an essential prerequisite for a successful bombing mission [particularly one mounted against a moving target] was close collaboration between air reconnaissance units and bomber units. Usually one or more bomber units were held on the ground on alert, ready to take off when the reconnaissance aircraft reported a suitable target.

There are many cases where German air units sealed off battle areas during the Second World War. During the Polish campaign in 1939, as a result of attacks on rail targets, the Poles were able to bring into action only 37 infantry divisions, 11 cavalry and seven border guard brigades, of a total of 45 infantry divisions, 16 cavalry and 10 border guard brigades mobilised. During the Battle of the Radom Pocket[7] the Luftwaffe halted rail and road traffic in northern and eastern Poland, preventing the Poles from assembling a task force at Kielce. By 8 September the Luftwaffe had halted traffic on the major routes Poznan–Kutno–Warsaw, Krakow–Radom–Deblin, Krakow–Tarnow–Lvov and connecting roads between them. The rail routes were blocked by destroying depots, rail track and trains. As a result the Poles were forced to abandon the rail routes and head east by road. By continuous attacks on the latter the Luftwaffe prevented an orderly retreat and the establishment of a defensive line west of the Vistula river.[8]

The success of the above air operations is confirmed in a report by General Kutrzeba, commander of the Polish Army of Poznan:

> Towards 1000 hours the enemy commenced vigorous air attacks against the bridges at Vitkovice. In terms of the numbers of aircraft committed, the severity of the attacks and the daring displayed, the enemy air operation was remarkable. Every movement, every troop concentration and all march routes were subjected to destructive air attacks . . . It was Hell on Earth. Bridges were smashed, fords were blocked, the anti-aircraft and part of the artillery forces were annihilated . . . Continuation of the battle would have been nothing but a matter of holding out. To have remained in position would have allowed the German Air Force to turn the place into a graveyard, since there were no anti-aircraft defences of any sort.

This statement from a Polish army commander confirms the decisive contribution of the Luftwaffe to the victory in Poland.

In the 1940 campaign in France, German air power was committed extensively against enemy communications with the aim of sealing off battle areas. At the start of the campaign, for example, Air Fleet 3 attacked French communications as far back as a line from Givet through Hirson, Laon, Rheims and Sainte-Menehould to Verdun, with the main emphasis on the area in front of Charleville–Sedan. As soon as the Luftwaffe established air superiority, air attacks to a depth of about 50 miles behind the front line struck moving troop columns, troop concentrations and rail routes.[9]

Situation reports from the Intelligence Division, Luftwaffe General Staff, on 15 and 16 May describe the operations by Air Fleet 3 to seal off the battle area. Units delivered continuous attacks in support of Army operations in the area Fumay, Châlons-sur-Marne, Revigny-sur-Ornain, Metz and Longuyon. In the Charleville–Stenay area west of the Meuse river, air units delivered powerful attacks on moving troop columns, troop concentrations, fortifications and traffic routes. Single- and twin-engine fighter units flew escort missions and fighter sweeps to maintain air superiority. In the Sedan–Charleville area alone, sixty-nine enemy aircraft were shot down in air combat. These continuous air attacks by day, and harassing attacks at night, prevented the timely movement of sizeable enemy forces. This provided effective support for German ground forces to advance into the Montcornet–Rethel–Attigny area.[10]

Strong forces from the other German air fleet committed in France, Air Fleet 2, were employed in similar manner:

Air Fleet 2 had the mission of supporting the advance by the Fourth Army [the main German assault army which was to punch through to the Channel coast] and covering the left flank in a line from Abbeville through Amiens and Laon to Rethel. Concurrently, the air fleet was to prevent a French withdrawal across the Somme river.

Attacks on rail targets made it difficult for the enemy to move reinforcements. The routes heading north-east, crossing a line extending from La Fère through Amiens to Abbeville and thus threatening the rear of the German spearhead forces, were attacked repeatedly. The bombing caused particularly serious damage to rail installations at Amiens and to the south of the city.[11] Between Revigny-sur-Ornain and Bar le Duc about thirty-three trains were halted.

These examples show that air support for the ground forces, by sealing off the battle areas, made a decisively important contribution towards victory in the French campaign. This was separate from the close tactical air support given to Army forces, described in a later section.

During the Balkan campaign, too, air attacks on enemy communications made an important contribution towards bringing it to a rapid and successful conclusion. In Yugoslavia, the after-action report by the Wehrmacht High Command[12] stated that, 'Through continuous action against the enemy communication and supply routes . . . the Luftwaffe did much to cause the disintegration of the Serbian Army.'

Following the campaign in Greece, the after-action report by the Wehrmacht High Command described the contribution made by the Luftwaffe in these terms:

Through the rapid defeat of the enemy air forces and maintenance of air supremacy throughout the campaign, the Luftwaffe made it impossible for enemy air action to disrupt [land] operations.

With exemplary cooperation the Luftwaffe supported the Army through constant close and long-range reconnaissance operations, through attacks by dive-bombers to help breach the main enemy lines of resistance and through day and night attacks on retreating enemy forces and their communications to speed up their disintegration . . .

Bombers and dive-bombers were particularly successful during attacks on shipping in Greek coastal waters. This hindered the withdrawal of the British forces and caused serious damage to British shipping.[13]

Once the Luftwaffe had neutralised the enemy air force in the first few days of the campaign in Russia, it shifted to supporting Army operations. For this purpose the bombers and part of the dive-bomber force were committed in attacks aimed at sealing off the battle area. Initially there were so many enemy columns on the move that the Luftwaffe had insufficient planes to attack them all, in addition to its other commitments and in particular that of rail interdiction.

In his study 'The Luftwaffe in the Eastern Theatre' (*Die deutsche Luftwaffe an der Ostfront*), General Plocher summarised the situation as follows:

> During the first few weeks of the campaign enemy troop movements made profitable targets for bombers. Moving in two, three or four columns abreast on a single road in close order, with motor and horse-drawn vehicles between the marching troops, they were easy prey for the bombers. (During the summer the ground on either side of the roads was used as a roadway, so that the roads were effectively up to 100 yards wide).[14]

In the first few months of the Russian campaign unbelievably large marching columns and troop concentrations were seen on the Russian side. However, unexpected difficulties limited the ability of Luftwaffe to attack these targets. The principal problem was a lack of sufficient bombs of the proper types. This seriously reduced the effectiveness of air attacks during this crucial period in the campaign. As a result the enemy had stronger forces available for the decisive battle before Moscow than would otherwise have been the case.

Another air mission during the first year of the Russian campaign involved the support of ground operations during battles of envelopment. During 1941 strong Russian forces were trapped in large pockets on seven separate occasions; German forces captured 2,256,000 Russian prisoners, 9,336 tanks and 16,179 artillery pieces. Initially the pockets were closed only by small armoured forces with weak contingents of motorised infantry. These had the task of containing the Russian troops until the main German infantry divisions arrived on foot. If led by an energetic commander, Russian troops could always find a point from which they could break out of the enveloping lines. The fastest and most effective way to seal these gaps would have been with paratroops. The German command did not have enough of these forces available, however, because after the heavy losses suffered during the capture of Crete the units had to be re-formed.

The task of the Luftwaffe during these battles was to frustrate moves by Russian reserves to relieve the trapped forces, and prevent Russian troops escaping through the German lines. In the latter case the Luftwaffe was only partially successful, however. Men often broke out through wooded areas or at night, when effective air attacks were not possible. As a result large numbers escaped from the pockets.

During the campaign in Russia, air attacks on troop concentrations and troops on the move played an important role. The Russians soon learned to restrict their movements to night, and to move forces in smaller units. During offensives, however, and particularly during the great Russian offensives launched after 1943, large troop concentrations and movements were often in evidence during the day.

As in earlier campaigns, air attacks on the Russian rail system commenced immediately after the start of the campaign. Because of the need to commit Luftwaffe forces to other missions, however, only rarely was the rail interdiction operation clearly defined. In the first year of the campaign one such concentration of effort was that in the area Smolensk–Bryansk–Gomel–Mogilev, in June 1941. Later, during the Battle of Kiev in July, forces from two air fleets were committed to operations in the area Kiev–Kazatin–Shepetovka–Korosten.[15]

Concerning the Bryansk area in June 1941, operations against the rail network were extended to include the area Gomel–Smolensk–Mogilev. The farthest point under interdiction was about 420 miles east of the tank units spearheading the German advance. As well as direct air operations in support of the drive towards Smolensk, Air Fleet 2 interdicted the rail system to a depth of 180 miles.[16] The interdiction of the rail system in these areas had an important bearing on operations in the Eastern Theatre. Indeed, three weeks after the campaign opened, the Wehrmacht High Command believed that the destruction of the rail system had deprived the enemy of the ability to carry out large-scale counter-attacks.[17]

The Battle of Kiev in 1941 involved a typical air action to seal off a battle area. On 21 August the Wehrmacht High Command ordered a 'concerted operation' to support forces on the left flank (Seventeenth Army and First Panzer Group) and those on the right flank (Second Army and Second Panzer Group) from the lines Kremenchug–Cherkassi and Gomel–Pochep, respectively. The operation involved four weeks of continuous combat action and culminated in the envelopment battle at Kiev. During this operation the Luftwaffe was to support the Army's advance and, by sealing off the battle area, prevent a possible Russian counterstroke. The operation reveals the varied types of mission required to be flown for the German Army. During the operation the emphasis shifted continuously between close air support missions and attacks on targets in the enemy far rear to seal off the battle area. By exploiting the flexibility and mobility of air power to the utmost, the [enemy] troops were strained to breaking point.[18]

The responsibility for air support missions was assigned to Air Corps V under General der Flieger Ritter von Greim in the southern area, and to Air Corps II under General der Flieger Loerzer in the northern area. The mission of the two air corps was to support the advance by ground forces and in particular by the armoured units spearheading the attack; to prevent enemy reinforcements from reaching the battle area from the east; and to disrupt enemy attempts to withdraw forces by road or rail.

Initially the Luftwaffe was well placed, because Air Corps II had recently moved into airfields close to the front. These were close to the important Kursk–Konotop–Kiev rail route used by the Russians, so bombers could make repeated attacks on this route each day. Operating from airfields south-west of Kremenchug, Air Corps V also had the Karkhov–Poltava–Kiev rail route within easy striking range. In executing their mission the two air corps made concerted attacks in support of the Army when the latter needed to break through fortified positions, force river crossings or resume the advance after a halt.

Whenever the tactical situation on the ground allowed, the air attack switched to communications targets in the far enemy rear. The systematic rail interdiction plan, coupled with another to attack columns moving along roads, effectively sealed off the battle area.

Between 1 and 11 September Air Corps V committed relatively weak forces to interdict the rail route from Karkhov through Poltava into the pocket area. Also, it attacked routes leading west through Karkhov. On 10 September, when First Panzer Group commenced its advance, Air Corps V shifted the focus of its attacks to targets inside the pocket. The aim was to prevent Russian reserves from moving into the battle area. Once the pocket was sealed off, Air Corps V units began a vigorous interdiction campaign against rail routes to the south-east of Karkhov. Flown to a depth of 180 miles from the front line, these operations prevented the movement of Russian reinforcements and matériel from the rear areas.

To protect the flank of Second Panzer Group, Air Corps II carried out rail interdiction operations against the Bryansk–L'gov route, routes in the Bryansk area and the Kiev–Kursk route. From 11 September, after forward elements of Second Panzer Group reached a point close to the latter, the focus of air attacks shifted to branch lines in the south. Then the weather deteriorated, and heavy rain hindered air operations for several days.

[When the weather allowed,] bomber formations delivered attacks from altitudes of between 6,600 and 13,200 feet. However, most of the attacks were by small units of between two and four aircraft, flying armed reconnaissance at low altitude. This was due partly to the changeable weather conditions, and partly to the bomber crews' aggressive spirit and their complete confidence in their superiority [over the enemy]. When attacking rail targets the primary target was the rolling stock. During crucial periods in the battle, for example on 8 September, units flew up to fifty strikes against locomotives and trains. On occasions night attacks were directed against busy rail depots, for example that at Karkhov on the night 15–16 September.

It has not been possible to discover the extent of the permanent damage inflicted on the Russian rail system. In the areas under attack there were few man-made structures, so there was little chance to inflict lasting damage. However, reports mention numerous trains stopped and several derailed. While the effects of individual air attacks were not always great, the cumulative effect of these operations was considerable. The Russians were unable to maintain traffic schedules or move essential supplies to the troops inside the pocket, nor could they withdraw troops from a pocket that was closing. At some points the Russians were successful in moving reserves into the area from the outside, however. On 18 September, for example, Second Panzer Group came under attack from a Russian tank division and a cavalry division, both of which had recently arrived in the area. The Russian High Command was unable to move in forces strong enough to influence on the course of the battle, however.

In retrospect it should be asked if these results could have been secured at less cost with, instead of the thousands of individual attacks on sections of rail tracks, a few heavy attacks on rail junctions in the enemy rear.

The scope of air operations in the first six months of the Russian campaign is evident from figures taken from an after-action report by Air Corps II. This stated that between 21 June 1941 (the date the campaign opened) to 13 November 1941 the air corps flew 3,579 rail interdiction missions and achieved the following results:[19]

> Rail tracks cut at 1,736 points
> Number of trains destroyed, 159

Number of trains damaged, 1,584
Number of locomotives destroyed, 304
Number of locomotives damaged, 103

Most of the trains attacked were carrying ammunition, which exploded; other trains were set on fire. In addition, the air corps attacked trains being loaded or unloaded.

Although 1941 was the peak year for interdiction operations against the Russian rail system, these operations continued with varying intensity for the remainder of the war. Later attacks did not achieve results as successful as those in 1941, however.

The Russians soon learned to exploit the hours of darkness and periods of bad weather to move rail traffic.[20] They also kept repair teams and stocks of replacement matériel at several points along the routes. This enabled them to repair bomb damage in a surprisingly short time. One report observed that bomb damage to the rail system in the Karkhov area was repaired or bypassed within 72 hours. Traffic resumed 'on miles of tracks laid down on a landscape of bomb craters on the virgin soil, bypassing the destroyed tracks.' Another complicating factor for the Luftwaffe was the difficulty of destroying rail tracks in winter. When bombs struck the hard, frozen ground they often bounced off it and detonated harmlessly some distance from the track.

Because of these factors the attacks on rail tracks became progressively less effective. In 1942 the emphasis shifted to attacks on trains travelling by night in areas near to the front. As the war drew on and the Russian Air Force became progressively stronger, the Russians resumed daytime rail movements too. In the meantime the German ground-attack units had re-equipped with FW 190, and each Geschwader included one Staffel that specialised in rail interdiction missions. Since these planes carried only a few bombs they concentrated on attacking locomotives.

In 1944 the Army Rail Transport Division learned that the Russians were running short of locomotives. The Russians have the [Western] Allies to thank for preventing these attacks from securing decisive results. Thus, one American writer noted:

In the three and one-half year period [October 1941–May 1945] under consideration we delivered to the Russians 1,900 steam locomotives, 66 diesel oil locomotives, 9,920 flat cars, 1,000 dump cars, 120 tanker cars and 35 [rail cars for the transportation of] heavy machinery . . .[21]

Rail interdiction operations resumed in the summer of 1944, employing specially trained units. The 9th Staffel of Bomber Geschwader 3 [equipped with Ju 88s] and the 14th Staffeln of Bomber Geschwader 27 and 55 [both equipped with He 111s] were assigned to Air Corps IV for operations against rail targets. This force achieved satisfactory results until fuel shortages forced its deactivation at the end of 1944.

In contrast to previous rail interdiction tactics [which concentrated on sections of track or trains moving over them], it was now decided to attack rail depots. These had previously come under air attack, sometimes with good results. For example, on 14 July 1941 units of Air Corps V destroyed the depot at the important rail junction of Bakhmach (on the Kiev–Kursk route) with approximately 1,000 rail trucks.[22] Major damage was also done to the Vyazma rail depot which, according to prisoners' statements, rendered it inoperable for fifteen days following the attack.[23]

Only in 1944 was it decided to change from pin-prick attacks on rail targets to concentrated attacks by massed forces against the larger targets. This may have been due to the fact that worthwhile targets lay far in the enemy rear, that the Luftwaffe lacked long-range escort fighters and that bomber units were inadequately trained [or equipped] for night-time operations.

Between 27 March and 22 July 1944 Air Corps IV dispatched large forces to attack Russian rail depots on twenty occasions. Some targets were attacked as many as six times. Bomber Geschwader 55, one of three such Geschwader assigned to Air Corps IV, reported that between 27 March and 5 May 1944 it flew 3,164 rail and road interdiction missions [almost certainly that figure related to sorties rather than missions].[24]

During the campaigns in Poland and France the destruction of bridges contributed to the success of ground operations. In the opening stages of the Russian campaign this was also true. As early as 1941, however, the strengthening of the defences around bridges made air attacks increasingly difficult. Moreover, even large bridges were repaired within astonishingly short periods. For example, in 1941 the Army requested the destruction of the bridges over the Dnieper to prevent Russian forces withdrawing across the river. Dive-bombers damaged the large rail bridge at Bobruysk to such an extent that rail experts judged it would be unusable for a long time. Surprisingly, the bridge was back in use in a few days. Once the area came under German control it was learned that a special repair team arrived by train from Moscow soon after the attack. Working day and night under the supervision of a Communist Party official of ministerial rank, they quickly restored the bridge to a limited operating capability.

Thus, as the war continued, the German attacks on bridges often failed to secure decisive results. In 1945 the failure to destroy the Vistula river bridges by air attack was nothing short of tragic. In 1944 the Western Allies succeeded, through the destruction of bridges in France, in delaying the movement of German reinforcements into the invasion area. Presumably the failure of the Luftwaffe to accomplish similar success was due to inadequate German technology, coupled with the general inferiority of the Luftwaffe at the time.[25]

The possibility of using of bridge demolition teams dropped by parachute in the enemy rear was mentioned in Air Field Manual No. 16, paragraph 172. During the war the Luftwaffe sometimes used this method. In November 1942, for example, after the Western Allies occupied French North Africa, Commander-in-Chief Southern Theatre ordered an operation by paratroops to destroy bridges on the rail and road routes running along the Mediterranean coast. The supply system of the Western Allies depended on these routes. In the mountainous areas were numerous large man-made structures, several of which came under attack. The enemy repaired the damaged bridges quickly, leading the Army [in Tunisia] to cease these operations.

Post-war publications confirm the effectiveness of these operations, however. General Eisenhower's book *Crusade in Europe*[26] states that in February 1943 the 34th US Infantry Division was withdrawn from the front to protect the rail and road routes. Furthermore, the withdrawal of Free French Forces to assist with this task contributed to the American defeat at the Kasserine Pass. The German demolition teams comprised approximately 60 German and 20 Arab personnel. According to an aide to General Eisenhower, their operations led to the withdrawal of more than 100,000 Allied combat personnel from the front for guard duties. It had been a remarkably successful instance of the Luftwaffe providing indirect support for the Army.[27]

To sum up, it can be said that war proved that the doctrine for the conduct of operations to seal off battle areas was sound. Often the Luftwaffe was able to exert decisive influence on ground operations.

Before the war the Luftwaffe realised that, to be successful, interdiction operations had to produce lengthy interruptions in traffic. Large forces of aircraft were therefore necessary. Following wargames conducted before the war, it was calculated that a bomber Geschwader of three Gruppen was necessary to keep a rail route permanently out of use. This proved correct as far as the Eastern Theatre was concerned.[28] If more than one Geschwader was committed to interdicting rail routes, it was advisable to assign a Geschwader to each of these and not change the target before the mission was completed. This ensured that crews became intimately acquainted with the route, the man-made structures along it and other details.

The German High Command expected that an enemy would do everything possible to keep his railway systems operating. However, in Russia [it was a surprise when], a few months after the campaign opened, the enemy effected major repairs so rapidly.

On the question of rail interdiction, the German High Command was mistaken on one point. Luftwaffe doctrine rejected the idea of attacking large rail depots and, in the words of Field Manual No. 16,

> ... the large number of tracks at such depots offers adequate possibilities for detours even when several tracks are damaged or destroyed ... [moreover,] large rail depots are usually heavily defended and have the personnel and materials to repair damage quickly.

Before the war the German High Command considered rail interdiction in too restricted a way, namely that of halting enemy troop movements. Yet large rail depots were collecting points for rolling stock, and these should have been designated as targets. By destroying the rolling stock such attacks would slow the flow of men and supplies to the battle area. No rail system can function if its rolling stock and repair installations are destroyed. Also, large targets of this type were better suited to air attack than sections of track, trains or individual locomotives. In exceptional circumstances, however, the latter might be appropriate as targets.

Providing Direct Air Support for the Army

Even in World War I it was evident that, during ground battles, situations developed where the only way to provide rapid support for the Army was by direct air attacks. This led to the establishment of special air units for the purpose.

On 10 July 1917 infantry of the German Fourth Army in Flanders went into action accompanied by aircraft. The latter brought enemy positions under fire and generally assisted the attacking troops. This new form of air support had a significant effect, both in terms of the physical damage inflicted and in its impact on the enemy's morale. The Commanding

General of the Air Service ordered the formation of special ground-attack units (Schlachtstaffeln). For the rest of the war these operated over the battle area, attacking enemy infantry and artillery positions, reserves moving forward, transport units and supply dumps.

The German offensive in France in March–April 1918 saw the climax in the use of the new weapon. For the first time, air power could provide direct assistance for infantry advancing on enemy defensive positions. Also, the ground-attack Staffeln were highly effective as a reserve force. They could move rapidly to any part of the front that came under threat.[29]

It was obvious that, in a future war, situations might develop on the ground that could only be mastered with the assistance of air power. The need for such assistance might develop:

1. during army operations to help friendly forces to reach their objectives or, conversely, to prevent enemy forces reaching theirs;
2. at the beginning of a friendly offensive, to assist ground forces in operations to break through enemy fortifications:
3. during the initial stages of an airborne or amphibious operation, to provide necessary additional firepower before the arrival of heavy weapons on the ground;
4. in cases where the friendly ground forces were at a disadvantage because they had insufficient weapons of certain specialised types – i.e., anti-tank weapons;
5. because of the appearance of certain types of enemy weapon, for example tanks or rocket projectors, in areas closed to friendly artillery observation, or where, owing to their small size and/or high mobility, they could be destroyed only by aimed direct fire.

German air doctrine preferred to employ air power in attacks on large targets in the enemy rear, because of the prospect of more profitable results from such attacks. However, it did not reject the idea of employing air power over the battle area under certain conditions. The revised (1940 edition) of Air Field Manual No. 16 stated:

Strong Luftwaffe forces can be committed during important ground battles. The method of cooperating with the Army will vary with the current situation, time factors, the nature and objectives of the mission, terrain conditions and the strength and nature of the forces available. No fixed pattern exists. The defining requirement is that the mission should produce important results for the Army. Thus bombers should strike at targets whose neutralisation will best serve the interests of the Army, or do most to thwart the enemy plans. The more closely the opposing armies are locked in battle, the greater the effectiveness of bombing attacks on areas near the battle front.

However, the above statement is qualified by the statement that air attacks on enemy forces in good tactical positions

. . . are usually unlikely to produce results commensurate with the effort expended, although such action might be required in special circumstances.

Those restrictions did not apply to air attacks made at the beginning of a ground offensive. In such cases the enemy troops would usually be badly shaken by the preparatory artillery bombardment. With their movements restricted by the advance of friendly ground troops, they were [by definition] not in good tactical positions. The Manual also placed limits on the participation of air units in action over the battlefield:

Air action [against targets] within the range of friendly artillery fire is justifiable only in cases where the artillery is unable fully to accomplish its mission.[30]

Air Manual No. 16 gives the impression that its authors felt that, although the air action over the battle area might be necessary, this should be the exception rather than the rule. Nevertheless, the Luftwaffe High Command realised that it was necessary to have single-engine ground-attack units available for missions over the battle area. In order not to jeopardise the build-up of other units, the ground-attack force was restricted to a single experimental Gruppe belonging to the Lehrgeschwader (Tactical Development Geschwader).[31] This Gruppe was formed to gather experience in this type of operation and develop tactics.

The Spanish Civil War showed the value of ground-attack units as a means of providing direct air support for the Army. These units were to concentrate at the point of focus (Schwerepunkt) in the battle, to support the advance of spearhead units. The soundness of this view was vindicated in the campaigns in Poland and France. Under General von Richthofen, the ground-attack units opened the way for the armoured units spearhead-ing the German advance. These attacks became an integral part of the pattern of Blitzkrieg. Moreover, the arrangement left offensive air force [i.e. bomber] units free to hit the targets best suited to their capabilities, namely large targets in the enemy rear.

At the beginning of the Russian campaign the clear-cut division of responsibilities [outlined in the previous paragraph] changed. The enor-mous frontage in the Eastern Theatre meant that often the Army had more than one point of main effort. The forces under General von Richthofen had expanded into a full air corps [Air Corps VIII], yet they were still not strong enough to provide support for more than one battle area.

[As the campaign in the East wore on,] the German Army became weaker, particularly in terms of effective anti-tank weapons. This led to increasing demands for direct air support, forcing the Luftwaffe to depart further from its doctrinal principles regarding the employment of air power. Another factor contributing to this development was the shift to a three-front conflict. Luftwaffe units were also committed against Britain and in the Mediterranean Theatre, which seriously reduced the number available for the Eastern Theatre.

When the German army units confronted stronger enemy forces, they could make good progress only when they had effective air support. After the Russian campaign opened, the advancing armoured forces required heavy support from the Luftwaffe.[33] An infantry regimental commander summed up his feelings in these words:

> Tanks in the lead, artillery in the rear and aircraft overhead – only then will the infantry advance to the attack.[34]

The Luftwaffe High Command viewed with mixed feelings the gradual move from providing indirect air support to the Army to providing an increasing proportion of direct-support missions. Had this been only during the relatively brief periods when the Army was engaged in important battles, it might have been justifiable. Yet even during quiet spells Army commanders insisted on having air power available to strike at targets. Often they needed to conceal their own weaknesses in terms of troop numbers and weapons.

The effect of this was to make Luftwaffe operations increasingly dependent on Army requirements. The extent to which the Luftwaffe High Command accepted this as inevitable is evident from the following comment from Generalfeldmarschall Kesselring:

> I instructed my Air Force and flak generals to consider the wishes of the Army as my orders, without prejudice to their subordination to me, unless serious air interests made compliance seem impracticable or detrimental. My commanding officers and I prided ourselves on anticipating the wishes of the Army, and carrying out any reasonable requests as quickly and as completely as we could.[35]

Targets of particular importance to the Army were often moving and/ or fleeting targets, for example advancing enemy infantry, guns on the move, tanks, ammunition transport columns and enemy reserves. In special circumstances it was also important to attack stationary and fortified targets, for example infantry and artillery positions and bunkers. Other categories of targets included bridges, command posts and signals centres. A characteristic common to most of these targets was their small size, which made them difficult to attack from the air.

Early in the war it was usual to commit only single-engine dive-bombers or ground-attack planes to missions in the battle area. Often these aircraft flew at low altitude to find and identify their targets. In the battle areas the enemy had dense concentrations of weapons, many of which could be used to engage aircraft. As a result these planes came under strong fire from the ground.

Multi-engine aircraft taking part in these operations presented large targets for ground fire and incurred heavy losses. Because of this, multi-engine [i.e. bomber] units were employed over the battle area only in exceptional circumstances. At the beginning of a ground offensive, for example, they might support the initial infantry attack on an enemy position. Later in the war the recurrence of critical situations on the ground led to their commitment more frequently over the battle area.

The provision of direct air support in the battle area created a need for special liaison teams, to avoid air attacks falling on friendly troops. The best cooperation was obtained when the tactical echelons of the Army and Luftwaffe headquarters were located side by side. General von Richthofen, commander of the only really large close support force available to the Luftwaffe, often [moved his headquarters to join that of the army commander] during critical situations.

At the beginning of the Russian campaign the other German air corps [i.e., other than von Richthofen's Air Corps VIII] furnished large-scale air support missions beside their primary bombing tasks. During the rapid German advances in 1941 these headquarters were unable to handle both responsibilities simultaneously without detriment to one of them. [Typically,] an armoured unit requiring direct air support might have broken through the Russian line of defence and be advancing into enemy territory. Following the armoured and motorised units, often as much as 48 miles behind, came the [German] non-motorised divisions advancing on foot. The tactical air support units, operating from hastily constructed field airstrips some distance behind the infantry, had to keep up with the advance. Time and again Russian troops penetrated the flanks between the [armoured spearhead units and the follow-up forces], so that often there were no secure [i.e. landline] signal communications between them.

Since they were also responsible for the direction of operations by bomber units, which used large airfields and supplies brought in by rail, the air corps headquarters had to establish special tactical air support units [to control that aspect of operations].

In May 1941 a Luftwaffe Tactical Bulletin stated that the tactical air support commander and his staff 'should be located in the immediate vicinity of the headquarters or command post of the army command to be supported'. Only then could the air support commander conduct effective operations. During the large-scale German offensives in the Eastern Theatre in 1941 and 1942 this produced good results. However, a continuing problem in the Eastern Theatre was the scarcity of adequate housing accommodation [caused by the 'scorched earth' policies adopted by both sides when they withdrew]. This often made it difficult for the air fleet and the army group headquarters to be located close together. The Wehrmacht High Command directive established that it was a Luftwaffe responsibility to maintain contact with the Army, so that the Luftwaffe had to furnish the necessary liaison personnel.

There were other reasons why air corps commanders often found it impossible to move their tactical staffs beside the army command headquarters they were supporting. Usually an air corps supported two or three field armies, with as many as twenty army corps operating on a frontage of up to 240 miles. With the frequent changes of main effort it was essential for the air corps to have direct communication (if possible by landline) with its airfields. Rarely was it possible to establish landline communications with the army corps in an area of main effort. This was possible only in exceptional cases where attack operations were planned well beforehand in otherwise quiet sectors of the front. Towards the end of the war the introduction of radio telephony [in place of the Morse systems] gave the air corps tactical staffs greater opportunities for flexibility in their operations.

In 1943 the tactical air support commands were disbanded, since offensive operations were no longer being staged on a large scale. With fierce fighting all along the line, each air corps had to support two or three armies. The focus of main effort shifted frequently and over great distances. Only exceptionally was the tactical air support command located beside the headquarters of the army corps it supported. Instead, the air liaison teams were responsible for keeping the air fleet headquarters informed of the current ground situation and the Army's plans.

In World War I it was customary for the air forces to attach air liaison officers to the army divisions operating in areas of main effort. These officers kept the officer directing air operations informed on current developments on the ground, the location of forward lines and Army intentions. To make them independent of wire communications, such liaison officers had their own wireless stations and the personnel necessary to operate them.

During the Spanish Civil War the German Command used Heinkel 51s in ground-support operations, directed by liaison teams assigned to the Army. Oberst von Richthofen, then commanding the German Condor Legion in Spain, employed radio teams with signals officers specially trained for the purpose.

During preparations for the campaign in Poland, von Richthofen, now a general, commanded the Special Purposes Air Command (Fliegerfuehrer zur besonderen Verwendung) directing the operations of air units supporting the Army. He organised four teams of the type described above, designated Air Signal Detachments (Luftnachrichtenverbindungstrupps). These detachments maintained close contact with the Army, essential for the execution of air support missions in the battle area. Two detachments were each equipped with an armoured reconnaissance car fitted with radio, so they could accompany commanders of armoured divisions.

The French campaign saw a greater use of these detachments and they were considered indispensable. As a result, during the preparations for the Russian campaign, the number of such units was increased further. The Air Signal Liaison detachments, as they were now known, consisted of a Luftwaffe signals officer with special training, a driver and four radio operators. Each detachment had a two radio sets which it maintained in operation continuously. For the Russian campaign the detachments assigned to armoured units had armoured vehicles, sometimes tanks, fitted with the appropriate radio equipment. Administratively these detachments were assigned to the nearest appropriate air unit headquarters, usually at air corps level. The air corps, air division or other air command responsible for the direction of air support controlled the air liaison detachments assigned to army commands in its area. At the start of the Russian campaign each army corps, and in exceptional cases army division, operating in areas of main effort had its own air liaison detachment. As the tactical situation became more difficult, with more rapidly changing areas of main effort, most army corps in the Eastern Theatre had one such detachment.

An air liaison detachment reported to its air corps anything special that occurred in that part of the front, whether in the air or on the ground. Also, at set intervals it reported the location of forward troop positions to update the ground situation map at air corps headquarters.

Unless the focal point for air operations was in its operational zone, an army corps could not send requests for air strikes through its air liaison detachment. The proper procedure was for the army corps to forward such requests to its superior army headquarters, where the request was weighed against those from other areas.

Early in World War II the air liaison detachments sometimes moved to forward observation posts. Occasionally they passed directions by radio, to assist air units to attack targets that were difficult to detect from the air. Usually, however, the most suitable locations for such posts were far from the detachment's assigned army headquarters. Thus, if a critical situation developed on the ground, contact between the army command post and the supporting air command was liable to suffer disruption. Yet it was during such situations that air support was most needed. Another weakness of the system was that the officer commanding the air liaison detachment usually lacked the training to control an air strike properly.

To overcome this problem the Luftwaffe established forward air control detachments to direct air strikes on to ground targets. Air corps headquarters instructed, by radio, the dive-bomber forward air control detachments (and later the ground-attack forward air control detachments) to move into the battle area to direct planned air strikes. The detachment took up a position from which it could observe the targets specified by the local infantry or artillery commander. On arrival over the area the air unit established radio contact with the detachment and was directed on to the target. Other methods used to identify ground targets included coloured smoke shells fired by the artillery and cloth directional signals laid out on the ground.

Later, when the air situation became difficult in the Eastern Theatre because of the strength of the Russian Air Force, forward air control detachments also worked with the fighter force. Assigned to local fighter commands, these detachments served in areas that were a focus for friendly or hostile air activity. If the general commanding the air corps went to the front to direct an operation personally, he transmitted orders to his aircraft via these control detachments.

Avoiding 'Friendly Fire' Casualties

The danger of bombs striking friendly troops was particularly acute during a rapid ground advance, or when bombers flew high-altitude bombing missions over the battle area. Consequently bomber attacks over the battlefield were authorised only if there were easily recognisable landmarks [for example, a river] to assist crews to find the target. During air attacks intended to breach enemy defences, it was essential to designate a line of salient terrain features as boundaries to prevent bombs falling on friendly forces. It was not normal German practice to withdraw troops as a protective measure during [friendly] air strikes.

When the ground situation became fluid it was particularly difficult to prevent bombs falling on friendly troops. One unsuccessful attempt to solve the problem used a rigidly fixed 'bomb line' [inside which no target was to be attacked unless crews were specially briefed, but beyond which any target could be treated as hostile] during a ground advance. During the campaign in France a new bomb line was established each day, for the following day. This proved a serious disadvantage, however. With the rapidly changing situation on the ground, the bomb line was often passed in a short time. Then the troops had either to halt their advance or risk being attacked by their own air force. If, on the other hand, the German forces were held up by enemy resistance or came under attack from enemy troops, the air force could not attack enemy troops or positions on the friendly side of the bomb line.[36]

The rapid advance of armoured forces at the start of the Russian campaign again illustrated the impracticability of establishing rigid bomb lines. This practice ceased in the late summer of 1941. Under the new system, if there was uncertainty regarding the identity of ground troops, as the air unit arrived over the target area it was to signify its intention to attack by firing flares. German troops were then to identify themselves by smoke signals or firing flares. Vehicles carried cloth identification signals that could be draped over them. If the situation on the ground remained unclear, the air unit was to attack an alternative target. These arrangements might also benefit enemy aircraft moving in to attack, but in 1941 that did not matter because the Luftwaffe held air superiority. The colours of the signals changed every few days, to prevent their use by the enemy. The use of smoke and flare signals proved satisfactory and they could be recognised even at high altitude. In particularly difficult situations, however, it still proved impossible to prevent bombs from falling on friendly troops.[37]

Decision Regarding the Nature of Air Support Required

As mentioned earlier, Wehrmacht High Command directives ordering air support for the Army did not specify whether this should to take the form of attacks to seal off the battle area or direct air support over the battlefield, or a combination of the two. Usually this was settled at air fleet/army group level. The basic principle was that air power should be used only in one area of main effort at a time, within the army group's zone of operations. This implied that of the two or three armies controlled by the army group headquarters, only one could receive air support. The only exception was when an air fleet had two high-level commands (air corps, air division, or other air command) each controlling several air units.

Usually agreement regarding the type of air support was reached at a lower command level, for example between the supporting air corps and the army to be supported. If direct air support was required over the battlefield, the appropriate army would inform the air corps which of its corps was to be supported. Once the army corps headquarters had been designated, it could if it wished delegate its powers to a division under its control. The air attack missions were then flown as laid down in paragraph 125 of Air Field Manual No. 16:

> ... the commanding officer directing ground operations will define the purpose of the air action, while the air corps will direct the execution of the air mission.

Once the preliminary arrangements were complete, requests for air strikes went from the army corps (or the nominated division) to the air corps. Mobile battlefield targets remained visible for only a short while, so it was important to keep as short as possible the time between detection of the target and the air strike. During a critical situation air units were held [on the ground] ready for immediate action. To allow flying personnel to have their necessary rest, however, alerts which called for units to take off at very short notice were to be ordered only if the units would soon go into action. Units that were placed too often on alert, when no action followed, usually reached a state where they did not take such alerts seriously. Then, when they were needed in a hurry, the preparations for take-off often took an exceptionally long time. To prepare for all contingencies, often it was sufficient to hold only part of a unit on immediate alert.

When bomber units were sent over the battlefield, they usually took twice as long as single-engine ground-attack or dive-bomber units to get airborne. Thus, the timely issue of orders was very important. Warning orders gave the unit time to make the preparations that took longest, for example refuelling and bomb-loading, and gave it an approximate time of take off. The operational order [for the air attack] contained information on the tactical situation on the ground at the target, the air situation, the current weather conditions and the forecast weather. Targets had to be designated with care and precision. It was essential to use large-scale maps, if possible 1:25,000 or 1:100,000. It was advisable to state the purpose of the mission, in case the unit had to attack an alternative target. As far as possible, details concerning the execution of the mission were left to the air unit commander.

Critical situations on the ground often required that missions be flown soon after daybreak. Usually that was before the air unit had received adequate information on the target and the weather conditions over the battlefield. In such cases it was advisable for the air unit to carry out its own target and weather reconnaissance. The unit sent an armed reconnaissance mission with two or three planes to the target area, whose crews passed the necessary tactical information to their unit by radio. Having made their reports, these aircraft were free to attack any suitable targets they found in the target area.

If a fighter escort was necessary, then the precise location, the altitude and the time of the rendezvous had to be stated. Usually only dive-bomber units received fighter escort. Ground-attack units had limited training in air combat and could protect themselves, with one Staffel providing top cover while another attacked the assigned target. If there was heavy defensive fire, it was sometimes necessary to assign part of the attacking force to hit the anti-aircraft gun positions. Sometimes it was possible to arrange for friendly artillery to engage the enemy anti-aircraft batteries while the air strike was in progress.

During the approach flight the air unit maintained radio contact with base. Any changes in the air or the ground tactical situation, or modifications to the mission order, were transmitted to the unit from its ground control station. If the air strike was directed by a ground controller in the battle area, the air unit established contact with the appropriate detachment which then directed it to the target. Usually the ground forces received no notification of the type of mission or its timing, since it was unlikely that such information would reach troops in the battle area in time. Agreements regarding the precise timing of an air strike were arranged beforehand only if the plan provided for ground forces to exploit the effects of the air strike. In special circumstances the attacking air units might have a bomb-release schedule that was coordinated with the ground artillery fire plan. After the air unit landed, the local air operations officer reported the results of the strike to air corps headquarters. If further missions were required, the report included information on when the unit would again be ready to take off and the number of aircraft available.

A few examples selected from the voluminous records available on the subject will illustrate points made in the above discussion. On 13 May 1940, the fourth day of the campaign against France,[38] the German Army High Command decided to launch an assault crossing of the Meuse river at Sedan. This surprise movement would enable armoured units to breach the main French line of resistance. Air support had a decisively important role in the operation. The orders to the 1st Panzer Division to cross the Meuse contained the following information on the air support operation:

> On 13 May the point of main effort of our Western offensive lies in the sector of Group von Kleist. Almost the whole of the Luftwaffe will support this operation. By means of uninterrupted attacks spread over eight hours the French defences along the Meuse will be smashed. This will be followed by an assault crossing of the river by Group von Kleist at 16.00 hrs and the establishment of bridgeheads.[39]

The army support mission included close support for troops on the battlefield, and also indirect air support to seal off the battle area. Regarding the air support for the army operation at Sedan, a Luftwaffe intelligence report stated:

> Continuous attacks by strong forces in a confined space neutralised the enemy defences and prevented enemy forces from launching a counter-attack. That allowed for the spearhead units of two armoured divisions and an infantry brigade to cross the Meuse river at two separate points between Charleville and Sedan.
>
> The drive through the enemy fortifications at Mezières and Sedan was carried forward to a depth of 12 miles in a southerly direction, then our forces crossed the Ardennes Canal heading west. Under pressure from the German drive, which had strong air support, the enemy troops are retreating in disorder ...

Of the many occasions on which air power was employed against permanent fortifications, the operation against Sevastopol in June 1942 merits special mention. The fortress had been built according to the latest experience and employed the most modern methods of construction then available. This presented entirely new and difficult problems for the attacking air force. Action had to be taken to destroy armoured gun batteries of the heaviest type and other fortifications. There were innumerable bunkers and field defensive works, with a maze of trenches and troop positions built into the walls of rocky canyons.

The operation required careful preparation by the Luftwaffe and the Army. In November 1941 the fortress was enveloped on the land side. Air reconnaissance recorded all permanent and field fortification works, artillery and mortar positions, alternative positions, anti-tank ditches, assembly areas for reserves and command posts. For the planning of air attacks this provided the best possible material for Air Corps VIII, which had been moved into the Crimea from the central sector because of its experience in the type of operations required. In the execution of missions against Sevastopol, the air corps was responsible directly to Commander-in-Chief Luftwaffe. The Air Force units available for the operation comprised 390 bombers, dive-bombers and fighters, which corresponded to 250–300 sorties per day.

The attack plan called for four days of uninterrupted air attacks and artillery fire against the Russian fortifications, to precede the infantry attack. The fire plan provided for the following:

1. at the same time as the first artillery bombardment, the air force was to attack enemy reserves positioned outside artillery range;
2. twin-engine bomber units were to mount day and night attacks against supply installations in the far enemy rear, as well as airfields and shipping;
3. operating in concert with the artillery, air units were to neutralise the enemy artillery and mortar batteries;
4. air units were to destroy targets, such as coastal artillery batteries, which the ground forces could not attack or take under observation;
5. artillery reconnaissance aircraft were to keep enemy artillery positions under constant observation.

Headquarters Eleventh Army expected that, besides the destruction achieved, the air attacks would be effective in wearing down the morale of the enemy troops.

Favoured by good weather, the first air missions were flown on 2 June and the air attack continued according to plan until 6 June. On 7 June the infantry attack opened on the north flank. From the early morning dive-bomber units delivered continuous attacks on defensive positions in front of the advancing infantry. During this action it was found that the preliminary bombardment had failed to destroy the combat morale of the enemy troops. Also, most of the heavy fortification works in the outpost area were undamaged. The attack on the ground failed to reach the shore of Servernaya Bay.

The attacks in this sector continued until 20 June, the infantry inching their way forward. Dive-bombers, operating in the ground-attack role, helped prepare their path. Fighters attacked fortifications, artillery positions and troops using bombs and cannon-fire. Aircraft and crews flew as many as eight combat missions per day.

The severity of this fighting led the Army to request that the Luftwaffe devote itself exclusively to providing direct support for the infantry. Some individual actions had a decisive influence on the outcome of the battle. For example, dive-bombers scored two direct hits on the armoured turret at the 'Maxim Gorki' fortified position [two 30.5cm guns] which put the turret out of action.[40] This greatly assisted the advance on the right flank of the enemy position.

On 11 June the ground forces on southern flank joined in the attack. Here also the main emphasis in air operations was against targets immediately in front of the infantry. On 29 June the final thrust began into the heart of the fortifications. To keep the defenders' heads down and assist in breaking their resistance, there was a massive aerial bombardment. Every available aircraft, even reconnaissance planes, joined in two hours of concentrated bombing on the Sapun Hills to prepare the way for the infantry. Their attack took them to the summit of the hills, then they advanced rapidly to the west and the south-west. At a few points the exhausted enemy troops continued to resist, but not for long. Despite the bitter tenacity of its defenders, the fortress finally succumbed to the cumulative effects of massed air attacks and heavy artillery fire.

During operations in support of the attack on Sevastopol the Luftwaffe flew a total of 23,751 sorties and dropped 20,000 tons of bombs. Flying from bases close to their targets, sometimes units could complete missions within twenty minutes [that was the total time airborne, from take-off to landing]. By bombing targets immediately in front of the infantry and preparing the way for their advance, the Luftwaffe made a decisive contribution to the land battle.

The airborne assault operation to seize the island of Crete in May 1941 was another excellent example of air support for a land operation. Air Corps XI consisted of two divisions, one of paratroops and one of air-landed troops. For the operation there was a special air transport command with some five hundred Junkers 52 planes, to serve as troop-carriers and glider tugs.[41]

The airborne assault operation commenced on the morning of 20 May with landings on Maleme airfield, near Rethymnon and on Heraklion airfield. The task of neutralising the ground defences during the paratroop attack was assigned to the Air Corps VIII. This had a strength of three bomber Geschwader, a Geschwader each of dive-bombers, single-engine fighters and twin-engine fighters, and two Staffeln of reconnaissance aircraft. The bulk of these aircraft operated from airfields near Athens and on Peloponnisos; others flew from bases in the Dodecanese, or on Rhodes or Scarpanto. Single- and twin-engine fighter units provided cover for the landing operations. Simultaneously, other aircraft attacked enemy anti-aircraft artillery positions near the airdrop zones. The action to protect the initial assault landings was so effective that of about five hundred Ju 52s taking part only seven were lost. The first paratroops reached the ground soon after the targets had been bombed, so that the men could take cover in the newly created craters. Aircraft also bombed barracks and bivouac areas to prevent enemy reserves reaching the drop zones. Since the transport planes then available could not carry heavy weapons, Air Corps VIII had to provide the necessary fire support during the ground fighting that followed.

The provision of air support for an amphibious operation is best illustrated by the seizure of the Baltic Islands in September 1941. For this operation the Commanding General XXXXII Army Corps had command authority over the air and naval units involved. The Luftwaffe assigned to the operation three bomber Gruppen, a twin-engine fighter Gruppe, a single-engine fighter Staffel and three coastal reconnaissance Staffeln. Contrary to the Luftwaffe's wishes, the plan called for the initial landing on Muhu Island to take place during the early morning darkness on 14 September. That meant that the landings could have no direct air support until after daybreak.

In the event bad weather delayed the landings and a critical situation developed. Enemy artillery and anti-aircraft guns inflicted heavy losses among the assault boats. Flanking fire caused casualties as the infantry crossed the beach. The German supporting fire had little effect, because poor visibility hindered observation from the heavy gun batteries on the mainland. Only after air units had neutralised the enemy artillery batteries and had given direct air support was the infantry able to establish a beachhead. Continuing air support thwarted enemy attempts first to reinforce the garrison, then to evacuate it when the island was finally captured.[42]

The Russian counter-offensive in July 1943 offers a good example of the use of air support during an army defensive operation. The plan for the German Zitadelle offensive[43] had provided for the Ninth Army to form the northern prong in an operation to envelop the Russian forces around Kursk. Its mission was therefore to stage an all-out drive towards the south-east from the Orel river bulge. Before the offensive, the German High Command had foreseen the possibility of a Russian counter-attack and had realised the danger inherent in such a move. Two days before the German offensive began, Hitler addressed the commanding generals of the participating armies and corps near his headquarters in East Prussia. He spoke about the latent threat, and declared that if the Russians launched a counter-attack he would throw into action his last available aircraft to block it.[44]

The German Second Panzer Army was holding the Orel river bulge when the Ninth Army thrust to the south-east ran into difficulties. Then a Russian armoured brigade broke through the German defensive line and established itself across the only rail and road supply route to the two German armies. The threat appeared imminent of a catastrophe even greater than that at Stalingrad.

In fact the 1st Air Division in the Orel river bend area did receive large reinforcements after the Russian counter-offensive began. Reinforcements continued to arrive until Air Fleet 6 declared that it could not support further units. In a series of heavy air attacks the Luftwaffe succeeded in preventing a Russian breakthrough, though on several days this was threatened. These delaying operations enabled German ground commanders to make gradual withdrawals in some semblance of order, to straighten the front lines.

The final report on the Battle of the Orel River Bend described the 1st Air Division's achievement:

The figures showing the results achieved by the 1st Air Division in these actions are particularly impressive. It performed its mission resolutely, alternately providing support for the Ninth Army and the Second Panzer Army. As well as air combat missions, it provided indirect support for ground operations.

The air division, whose actions resolved several critical situations, flew a total of 37,421 sorties. It shot down 1,735 enemy aircraft, 1,671 by fighter action, for a loss of only 64 planes. In addition the air units put out of action 1,100 tanks, 1,300 wheeled and tracked motor trucks and other vehicles, and numerous artillery batteries.[45]

It dropped more than 20,000 tons of bombs on targets and inflicted heavy losses in personnel, railway rolling stock and supplies. During the Battle of the Orel River Bend units of the air division sometimes flew up to five or six missions in a single day.[46]

Events in previous campaigns had shown the need to concentrate forces when mounting an offensive. Drawing on those lessons, the German supreme command should have realised the importance of concentrating the available air power during operations to repel enemy offensives. As well as concentrating all available tactical air support units, it was necessary to break with the old system of distributing the available multi-engine bomber Gruppen among the various air fleets. If the supreme command had direct control over these air units, it would have had an effective instrument with which to exercise decisive influence at selected points. Admittedly this would have required a change in the existing command organisation, but this was long overdue.

The above paragraph does not imply that there should have been an increased emphasis on army air support operations. The requirement was for concentrated air attacks, as described, but only during the short periods when the ground tactical situation made them necessary. However, the German High Command failed to learn the obvious lessons of the Battle of Orel and, instead, it continued to spread air combat units far too widely.

It is undeniable that time and again German air power successfully neutralised enemy armour. The campaign in the West in 1940 proved that the aircraft was an effective weapon against tanks. Indeed, a well-prepared operation by armour could be halted through the use of air power. For example, as XIX Panzer Corps drove towards the Channel coast, General de Gaulle's armoured force, in the plain of Laon, struck the flank and penetrated to a considerable depth. German dive-bombers defeated the attack, and put most of the French tanks out of action.[47, 48]

In 1943 the introduction of anti-tank aircraft fitted with heavy cannon proved highly successful. On 8 July, during the Zitadelle offensive, the IVth Gruppe of Ground Attack Geschwader 9 repelled a surprise attack by a Russian armoured brigade against the rear flank of the Fourth Panzer Army. Commanded by Hauptmann Bruno Meyer, the IVth Gruppe comprised four Staffeln each with sixteen Hs 129 aircraft; each aircraft was fitted with an MK 101 30mm cannon. For about an hour the Gruppe sent relays of aircraft to attack the Russian force, which was halted and then forced to withdraw. With many Russian tanks and other vehicles on fire, the German Fourth Army continued its advance without interference.[49, 50]

As the war continued, the number of tanks deployed by the Russians on the Eastern Front continued to mount. Countering these was a matter of life and death for the German Army, which was short of effective anti-tank weapons. For the Luftwaffe, this was a mission it could not avoid.[51]

In spite of individual successes achieved in this area (Oberst Rudel, for example, destroyed 519 Russian tanks[52]), too few Russian tanks were being eliminated. Moreover, Russia's output in tanks continued to rise because the Luftwaffe did nothing, or practically nothing, to interfere with tank production. The Russians built an impressive 150,000 tanks[53] during the war, compared with 25,000 by the Germans.[54] In addition, the Western Allies delivered large numbers of tanks to Russia.

Initially the types of bombs available to the Luftwaffe for use against tanks were unsuitable for the purpose. A near miss, even within a few yards of a tank, usually did no damage at all. That situation improved with the introduction of the SD 4 anti-tank bomb with a hollow-charge warhead. However, these bombs, and also the newly developed anti-tank rockets for aircraft, reached front-line units too late to have any decisive effect.

In the circumstances obtaining in World War II, it has to be admitted that the support of ground forces on the battlefield was a valid mission of air power. This being the case, an appropriate command organisation and specialised combat units were necessary for the purpose. To produce telling results, it was essential to concentrate air power against enemy tank forces. Usually, within a specific theatre, large-scale ground operations were restricted to one or two sectors at a time. Thus the air operations could be focused on areas of main activity on the ground. Often this was not done on the German side. High-level army commands did their utmost to hold air units in their command zone, whenever there was a suggestion that forces be redistributed. Oberst Kusserow admitted as much in a post-war report issued in September 1954. At the beginning of the Russian campaign, he wrote, the focus of the main effort on the ground was also the focus for the concentration of air power. Later this principle was disregarded, with combat air units distributed across the front to the detriment of fighting efficiency and effectiveness. Usually this was in response to requests and demands from army commands, made on a scale that was impossible to justify from the standpoint of sound tactics or strategy.[55]

In discussing the basic requirement that air power should be used in a concentrated mass, it has to be admitted that a crisis might develop in a previously quiet sector of the front. Also, given the continual shortage of German reserves, such a crisis might cause a disastrous situation. Under such circumstances it was justifiable to leave a small tactical air unit, perhaps a Gruppe, in the command zone of each army group as a local emergency reserve. Apart from that, all other air units within each theatre of operations should be concentrated at the decisive point [or points].

On the Eastern Front, contrary to this basic principle, tactical air support units were distributed among the various sectors. Moreover, purely from a perceived need to keep them occupied, the units were continuously in action even when there was no chance of achieving useful results. This policy stemmed from the army commands, who felt that such continuous attacks would weaken the enemy. Most air fleet headquarters also pursued this policy. At the close of each day they would examine critically whether their available aircraft had been committed often enough 'in order to avoid the Commander-in-Chief Luftwaffe taking away units'. Their examination rarely considered whether the results were commensurate with the effort expended. For example, in a quiet sector of a front, enemy troops not engaged in ground combat could use their weapons against attacking aircraft. As a result the latter suffered excessive losses and achieved little. Moreover, due to the urge to keep air units in action, they were not allowed adequate time for rest or additional training. Unless units went to the rear to [re-form or] re-equip with a new aircraft type, they remained in action almost constantly. Moreover, throughout this time the air units failed to achieve decisive results in those areas where decisive ground actions were taking place.

The German side lacked a system by which each theatre of operations came under a joint command with a detailed insight into the situation along the entire battle front. Such a command should have had authority over both the army and the tactical air support units, and directed the operations of both. Instead, the air fleet in each theatre was under the Commander-in-Chief Luftwaffe, whose headquarters was far from the fighting fronts.

The various army groups came under the Army High Command or the Wehrmacht High Command. There too, the headquarters were too far from the various fronts for these top-level commanders to have precise knowledge of the situation at each one. Moreover, because of their other heavy responsibilities, these commanders could not give adequate attention to each of the battle fronts.

Theoretically, the commitment of bombers over the battlefield should have been authorised only in exceptional circumstances, for example, to create a breach in the enemy defences for attacking ground forces, or if there was an exceptionally grave situation for ground forces. What actually happened is evident from a report by the last commander of the Bomber Geschwader 1, Oberstleutnant von Riesen. In reality, he contended, the Luftwaffe came to be 'a means of combat of the army groups and armies'. Thus the ground forces came to look on all types of Luftwaffe units as a means of solving problems that were 'strictly the task of the ground-attack forces'.

This situation reached the point of absurdity when heavy bombers were dispatched singly to deliver low-level attacks on tanks [this happened in July 1944, when on express orders from Goering, Heinkel 177s were used in an unsuccessful bid to slow the Russian advance]. At the same time, those fighter units not dissipated in ground-attack missions had to battle with enemy forces that were greatly superior in numbers. 'This outcome,' von Riesen observed, 'was brought about by a command which had failed to grasp how valuable air power could have been in this war.' This wasteful and misconceived use of air power led to the loss of the war in the air, which in turn led inevitably to defeat on the ground.[56]

The problem of what could have been done to prevent this misuse of the bomber force will be addressed in the closing chapter of this study. The errors in organisation and employment were exacerbated by shortages of matériel. Often the Luftwaffe lacked the proper weapons for direct air support. At the beginning of the Russian campaign, for example, it failed to provide adequate supplies of fragmentation bombs. The lack of suitable weapons for anti-tank aircraft has been mentioned, and this lack was aggravated because German ground forces were also inadequately equipped in this respect.

It may well be that in a future war, the use of rocket weapons will reduce or do away with the need to commit air forces over the battlefield. For, generally speaking, that is an uneconomical way to use air power.

Notes to Chapter 4

1. Oberst Hans Jeschonnek, Chief of the Luftwaffe General Staff, 'General Observations on Tactical Operations', from a General Staff Tour Critique, June 1939, Karlsruhe Document Collection, F III 1. In February 1939 Oberst Jeschonnek had become Chief of the Luftwaffe General Staff, succeeding General Hans Stumpff in that post. In 1943 the demands of the office drove Jeschonnek to such despair that on 19 August he committed suicide.

2. This is an exaggeration. During 1942 and 1943 Soviet tank production was about 24,000 per year, or an average of about 65 tanks per day. However, the author's general point, on the value of attacking the tank production facilities, remains valid.—A.P.

3. The substance of paragraphs 162–177 [of Air Staff Manual No. 16] provided that in the circumstances of enemy concentration and regroupment, operations against transport networks must be in close cooperation with the Army. Combat operations against troop concentrations and other troop movements must be primarily a rail interdiction mission. A key factor is proper timing. The fact that part of the movement could occur by road and across country reduces the time available for attack. Exploitation of the hours of darkness makes timely detection and attack a difficult matter. Valuable results may be achieved through attacks against particularly important and large structures; targets of this type include river bridges, viaducts and tunnels. Timely recognition of a movement is possible only if all intelligence sources are fully exploited, and if constant air reconnaissance is maintained. If signs of a movement multiply, air reconnaissance must be employed to the utmost. Lack of night air reconnaissance must be compensated [for] by early morning and late evening missions. In urgent situations, air photo reconnaissance and interpretation must be complemented by visual observation and, in certain cases, by radio. Important factors of success are (a) in troop concentration movements, the distance behind the enemy lines at which rail track was destroyed, (b) in regrouping movements, the distance from enemy unloading points at which rail track was are destroyed. The attacks must interdict the entire movement, without any chance to re-route it. Particularly effective results can be obtained through the destruction of structures at points on which routes of the rail network converge. Destruction of the rail lines between rail depots is usually more easily achieved but less effective. In general, rail depots and rail junctions should not be targets for interdiction attacks. Attacks against moving railway trains, however, are effective. Generally speaking, attacks against loading and unloading operations do not offer much prospect of success. The results achieved in attacks on roads cannot be as great as those against the rail system.

4. A specimen is in Appendix 9, unpublished appendices of USAF Historical Study No. 163, Karlsruhe Document Collection.

5. John R. Deane, *The Strange Alliance* (New York, 1947), p. 93.

6. An example is in Appendix 11 in unpublished appendices of USAF Historical Study No. 163, Karlsruhe Document Collection.

7. Reference is to the Tenth Army's breakthrough to the Vistula and the Battle of the Radom Pocket, in which large Polish forces were effectively encircled by 12 September, resulting in the capture of 60,000 prisoners and 130 guns.

8. 'Der Feldzug in Polen in Stichworten' (The Polish Campaign in Brief), Records of Historical Division (8th), Luftwaffe General Staff, Karlsruhe Document Collection, G III 2C.

9. 'Der Einsatz der deutschen Luftwaffe waehrend der ersten 11 Tage der Frankreichfeldzuges' (Operations of the Luftwaffe during the First Eleven Days of the Campaign in France), taken from the daily situation reports of the Air Operations Section (Ic), Luftwaffe High Command, Karlsruhe Document Collection, G V 2c.

10. Ibid.

11. Ibid.

12. Cf. General der Flieger Paul Deichmann, 'Balkan-Feldzug des VIII Fliegerkorps' (The VIII Air Corps in the Balkan Campaign), Karlsruhe Document Collection, G VII 6.

13. Ibid.

14. An unpublished German monograph study in the Karlsruhe Document Collection. See also Generalmajor Hitschold, 'Die Entwicklung der Schlacht- und Sturzkampf-fliegerei waehrend des Kampfes in Russland' (Development of Attack and Dive Bombing Aviation during the Battles in Russia), Karlsruhe Document Collection; and 'Der Luftkrieg im Osten 1941' (The Air War in the East, 1941), Karlsruhe Document Collection.

15. 'Abschnuerung des Schlachtfeldes waehrend der Schlacht um Kiew' (Isolation of the Battlefield during the Battle of Kiev), taken from situation reports, Operations Staff, Luftwaffe High Command, Karlsruhe Document Collection, G VI 3b.

16. 'Der Luftkrieg im Osten gegen Russland 1941' (Air Warfare against Russia in the Eastern Theatre in 1941), Report, Military History Division (8th), Luftwaffe General Staff, Karlsruhe Document Collection, G VI 3a.

17. Generalleutnant Hermann Plocher, 'Unterstuetzung des Heeres durch die deutsche Luftwaffe im Osten 1941/42' (Support of the Army by the German Air Force in the East, 1941–1942; hereinafter cited as 'Unterstuetzung des Heeres'), Karlsruhe Document Collection, G VI 3a.

18. Ibid.

19. 'Das II Fliegerkorps im Einsatz gegen Russland vom 22.6.41–15.11.41' (The II Air Corps in Operations against Russia from 22 June to 15 November 1941), Karlsruhe Document Collection, G VI 3b.

20. Zantke, 'Eisenbahnjagdeinsatz schwerer Kampfverbaende im Operations-programm der deutschen Luftkriegsfuehrung, 1941' (Heavy Bomber Formation Attacks on Railroads in the Operational Programme of German Air Warfare, 1941), Karlsruhe Document Collection, G VI 3d.

21. Deane, *The Strange Alliance*, pp. 94–95.

22. These figures regarding the damage inflicted to the Russian rail system should be taken with a pinch of salt. The author employed the term 'destroyed' in the vague and imprecise manner beloved of military men. What did it mean? Were all those rail trucks smashed into small pieces? Were some of them repairable? Or had they simply blown on their sides so they could be lifted on to the lines with a crane? Probably it was a combination of all three. And many trucks with serious damage were cannibalised to

produce parts for re-assembled trucks. Certainly the attack did not deprive the Russian rail system permanently of one thousand trucks.—A.P.

23. Plocher, 'Unterstuetzung des Heeres', Karlsruhe Document Collection, G VI 3a.

24. More details on these operations are contained in the sources available in the Karlsruhe Document Collection, among them a report by the Luftwaffe Operations Staff, Intelligence Section/East (D), entitled 'Grossangriffe des IV Fliegerkorps auf S. U. Eisenbahn System in der Zeit von 27. 3 bis 5.5.1944' (Major Offensive of IV Air Corps against the Soviet Railroad System from 27 March to 5 May 1944), Karlsruhe Document Collection, G VI 6b.

25. The failures were not due to inadequate German technology. The German Lotfe was an effective high-altitude bomb sight, similar in operation to the American Norden. The Luftwaffe's attacks on bridges late in the war failed because of a lack of air superiority in the target area. During the bridge attacks in France a typical US raiding force comprised about twenty-five B-26 Marauder medium bombers delivering a pattern-bombing attack from high altitude. Each such force had a strong fighter escort. Several such missions were flown each day and important bridges were attacked repeatedly until they fell. From mid-1943, only rarely could the Luftwaffe mount set-piece bombing attacks like this by day. More usually the German attacks involved about a dozen fighter-bombers, which had to fight their way through to the bridge and carry out individual bombing runs when they got there.—A.P.

26. Dwight D. Eisenhower, *Crusade in Europe* (New York, 1948), p. 122.

27. It is interesting to note that the Luftwaffe's responsibility for airborne forces included units which today would be termed 'special forces'.—A.P.

28. Significantly, the author does not cite a single case where an entire bomber Geschwader was committed for any length of time to this mission. If it happened at all, it was a rare occurrence.—A.P.

29. Details given here are taken from Lieutenant-General von Hoeppner, 'Aus Deutschlands Krieg in der Luft' (The German War in the Air) (Leipzig, 1921). General Hoeppner was General Commanding Air Forces.

30. This is an important stipulation. With only a few rare exceptions, if the Army has artillery in range with the firepower necessary to destroy a target under observation, it can do so more quickly and at far less cost than can the Air Force.—A.P.

31. The Lehrgeschwader (later the Lehrdivision with two Geschwader) comprised separate Gruppen with single-engine fighters, twin-engine fighters, bombers and dive-bombers. Their task was to develop and refine operational techniques, and crews assigned to them had more flying experience than those in normal front-line units. After the start of the war these Gruppen went into action in the same way as normal line units, and as they suffered losses they lost their edge in effectiveness compared with the rest of the Luftwaffe.—A.P.

32. Personal experience of the author during an assignment in the Operations Branch of the Luftwaffe High Command, 1935–37.

33. 'Die Unterstuetzung des Heeres im Osten 1941 durch die deutsche Luftwaffe' (Luftwaffe Support of the Army in the East, 1941), Historical Division (8th), Luftwaffe General Staff), Karlsruhe Document Collection G VI 3d.

34. Plocher, 'Unterstuetzung des Heeres', Karlsruhe Document Collection, G VI 3a.

35. Field Marshal Albert Kesselring, *Kesselring: A Soldier's Record*, tr. by L. Hudson (New York, 1954), pp. 96–7.

36. The problem remains unresolved to the present day. In 1991, when Coalition forces mounted thrusts into Kuwait and Iraq there were unfortunate cases of troops being killed in 'friendly fire' incidents. As a result, during the final two days of the conflict, when the Iraqi forces were in full retreat, a large proportion of the fighter-bombers arriving over the battle area did not receive clearance to attack ground targets and had to return to base with their ordnance.—A.P.

37. Appendix 20 in unpublished appendices of USAF Historical Study No. 163, Karlsruhe Document Collection, consists of a letter from VIII Air Corps to Army Group Centre dealing with this subject.

38. General Heinz Guderian, *Panzer Leader* (New York, 1952), Appendix VI (XIX Army Corps Order No. 3, 13 May 1940), p. 478.

39. The campaign in the West has been covered in the unpublished manuscript by General der Flieger Wilhelm Speidel on the German Air Force in France and the Low Countries, 1939–40, in the Karlsruhe Document Collection.

40. This battery was located directly south across the narrow peninsula from Sevastopol itself. It formed the extreme right wing of the inner ring of defences around Sevastopol, as well as commanding the sea approaches to the city from the south and east.

41. A considerable amount of material is available on the operation in Crete in the Karlsruhe Document Collection (G VII 8, G VII 8a) and also in the unpublished manuscript by Major Pissin in the German Historical Monograph series on the conquest of Crete.

42. Unpublished manuscript in the German Historical Monograph series by General Hermann Plocher on the Luftwaffe in the campaign in the East.

43. Operation Zitadelle was conceived by the Wehrmacht, not as a major offensive looking toward complete victory but as a means of further wearing down the Soviet Union to the point where, as Field Marshal von Manstein put it, the Soviet Union 'would tire of its already excessive sacrifices and be ready to accept a stalemate' (Manstein, *Lost Victories*, p. 443).

44. Personal experience of the author, who was present as Commanding General, Air Division 1.

45. The loss ratio of 27 Soviet planes destroyed for each German aircraft sounds fanciful in the extreme. So does the claim of 1,100 tanks put out of action – that represented almost one-third of the tanks and self-propelled guns committed by the Red Army during that battle!—A.P.

46. 'Gefechtsbericht der 9 Armee und der 2 Panzerarmee uber die Schlacht im Orelbogen, 5 July–18 August 1943' (Combat Report of Ninth Army and Second Panzer Army on the Battle of the Orel Bend, 5 July–18 August 1943), Ninth Army High Command, Karlsruhe Document Collection, G VI 5a.

47. G. W. Feuchter, 'Entwicklung und Kriegsentscheidende Bedeutung der Luftkriegfuehrung im 2 Weltkrieg' (Development and Decisive Significance in War of

the Air Warfare Leadership in World War II), *Flugabwehr und Technik*, Vol. II (Feb. 1949), p. 30.

48. In this context it is important to define the meaning of the word 'tank'. Almost certainly the author was here using the term to describe all tracked vehicles, including half-tracks and supply carriers. During the early war period the maximum thickness of armour carried by the latter was about 10mm. Light tanks of the period weighed about 5 tons and had 15mm frontal armour. Medium tanks weighed about 12 tons and carried 30mm frontal armour. The relatively few and slow-moving heavy tanks of that period weighed 30 to 40 tons and carried frontal armour with a maximum thickness of 60mm or more. With the exception of the few heavy tanks, any of the vehicles described above could be knocked out or temporarily disabled by a near miss from a bomb of 500lb or larger detonating within about 30 yards. The famous Russian T-34 tank was a different animal altogether. This 28-tonner went into action in quantity in the autumn of 1941 and until the closing stages of the war it was the main battle tank used by the Soviet Army. Its frontal armour was 60mm thick, and cleverly angled to increase the degree of effective protection it gave. The 1944 model, the 32-ton T-34/ 85 carried 90mm frontal armour and 20mm armour over the least-protected areas. The tank had a high power-to-weight ratio, giving excellent cross-country mobility. Most important of all, it was built in vast quantities – 40,000 according to one source. The giant 46-ton Josef Stalin 2, in action at the close of the war, carried frontal armour 120mm thick, with 19mm armour covering the least protected areas. In discussing the vulnerability of tanks to air attack, therefore, it is important to consider the types of vehicle in question. Obviously the Soviet tanks deployed in quantity from the autumn of 1941, which became the bane of the German Army on the Eastern Front, were far more difficult to knock out from the air than those attacked earlier in the war.—A.P.

49. Report by General der Flieger Hans Seidemann, 'Das VII Fliegerkorps im Osteinsatz, 1943' (The VIII Air Corps in Operations in the East, 1943), 1943, Karlsruhe Document Collection, G VI 5a. General Seidemann was commanding general of VIII Air Corps at the time, with the rank of Generalmajor.

50. This action has often been cited as an example of a concentrated operation by anti-tank aircraft which destroyed a large number of enemy tanks. The various commentators fail to give exact figures for the number tanks claimed destroyed, however. In considering this action it is worth looking at two others in this category where similar claims were made by air units at the time: the Battle of the Falaise Gap in Normandy in August 1944, and the Battle of the Bulge in December 1944. The significant difference between the two actions fought by the Western air forces and that by the Luftwaffe was that in the former the battlefield was afterwards inspected to determine how many tanks had actually been destroyed by air attack. Afterwards, detailed reports were issued on the findings. In the Falaise Gap area 385 tanks and armoured vehicles were examined, following heavy air attacks on German units retreating from the narrow pocket. Of that total only thirteen tanks and self-propelled guns were found to have been knocked out by air attack weapons, eleven by rockets and two by bombs. (See 'Enemy Casualties in Vehicles and Equipment during the Retreat from Normandy to the Seine', Report No. 15, No. 2 ORS 21st Army Group). In truth, the 3in

rockets fired from RAF Typhoons were not really accurate enough to achieve much success against tanks; a fighter-bomber firing all eight rockets in a single attack had a less than 5 per cent chance of scoring one hit on a tank. During the Battle of the Bulge USAAF and RAF units claimed the destruction of 751 German tanks and armoured vehicles. In a subsequent examination of areas where aircraft had claimed 66 tanks and 24 other armoured vehicles destroyed, the teams found 57 tanks, 18 self-propelled guns and 26 other armoured vehicles abandoned. Of that total only four tanks, two self-propelled guns and one other armoured vehicle exhibited major damage caused by air attack. If that figure is extrapolated for the entire area of the Battle of the Bulge, the number of tanks and armoured vehicles destroyed from the air was less than sixty. (See RAF 2nd Tactical Air Force Operational Research Section Report No. 19, 'The Contribution of the Air Forces to the Stemming of Enemy Thrust in the Ardennes').

From the reports cited above, certain general conclusions can be made. The first is that main battle tanks of the mid-war period, like the German Mark IV, the Panther and the Tiger, were difficult targets to destroy from the air. Many attacks were made on them, but only a very small proportion of these inflicted major damage. A tank can be hit and it might even give off smoke, without having suffered mortal damage. No pilot was going to make a second pass through murderous flak to see if the tank really had been destroyed. Because of this, although no doubt pilots claimed tank kills in good faith, they usually overclaimed by factors in excess of ten to one. In the case of the Bulge action, for example, only seven per cent of the armoured vehicle kills claimed by pilots were confirmed by subsequent ground examination.

There is no reason to believe that the Soviet T-34 tanks were any easier to knock out from the air. Moreover, following the action near Kursk on 5 July 1943, the battle area was not in the hands of the German Army, so German inspectors could not examine the wrecked vehicles. In the absence of an account of the action from the Russian side, we cannot know for certain why the Russian armoured brigade broke off its advance and pulled back. For what it is worth, this editor regards the claim of large numbers of tanks destroyed during this action as 'not proven'.—A.P.

51. 'Panzer-Bekämpfung im Osten, 1943/44' (Combat against Tanks in the East, 1943/44), Karlsruhe Document Collection, G VI 5a.

52. For the reasons stated in note 50 above, this writer believes that the number of tanks that Rudel actually destroyed was substantially less than the 519 claimed. Only rarely could his tank kills be confirmed by ground inspection. During anti-tank operations Rudel flew a Ju 87 with two 37mm cannon under the wings.—A.P.

53. Wartime Soviet tank production was huge, but it was probably somewhat less than the figure quoted of 150,000. Other sources suggest that the figure was nearer 100,000 – still many times greater than the number of tanks the German Army could deploy on the Eastern Front.—A.P.

54. Eike Middeldorf, 'Taktik im Russland Feldzug' (Tactics in the Russian Campaign), Mittler und Sohn, (Frankfurt/Main).

55. Kusserow, 'Unterstuetzung', Karlsruhe Document Collection, F III 1.

56. Horst von Riesen, 'Die Luftwaffe – der hervorragende Faktor eines Krieges' (The Air Force – The Dominant Factor of War), *Flugwelt*, Vol. II (1955).

CHAPTER 5

Army Support as a Proportion of the Total Air Effort

To assess the share of the total air effort expended in support of army operations, it is necessary to divide this between those air actions to seal off the battle area and those to provide direct support over the battlefield. Although the available sources[1] do not give detailed information on this subject, they provide some useful pointers. Also, they reveal the extent to which army support operations led to the neglect of other air power missions that were of equal or greater importance.

The Polish Campaign, 1939

In a study entitled 'Survey of German Conduct of Air Warfare' (*Ueberblick ueber die deutsche Luftkriegfuehrung*), the 8th (Military History) Division of the Luftwaffe noted:

> Over Poland the independent air force made its first appearance as a weapon that could decide the outcome of a campaign. In this role its mission required a clearly defined concentration of effort, to secure the rapid defeat of the enemy. It was required to carry out the following tasks:
>
> *a.* The destruction of the Polish Air Force, its ground service organisation and the Polish aircraft industry.
> *b.* The support of army operations, to ensure a rapid breakthrough and a speedy advance by the ground forces.
> *c.* Attacking Polish military installations and armament factories in the Warsaw area.

For these tasks two air fleets were available, with a total strength of 1,558 first-line aircraft.[2] Early in September 1939, 483 aircraft were committed to operations to counter the enemy air force. During the drive to the Vistula–San line units flew 4,806 sorties in indirect army support missions. During the battles at the border and the fighting that followed, units flew 3,740 sorties in direct air support missions. Thus the ratio of aircraft employed in strategic missions, compared with those employed in direct air support missions for the Army, was 5:4.

[At the start of the war] the Polish Air Force had 400 first-line aircraft available. Within two days the Luftwaffe had established air supremacy over Poland, and attacks on the Polish Air Force compelled it to operate from emergency airfields and rendered it less effective. Polish commanders were then unable to employ their remaining air units in a coherent pattern of operations. Because of these factors the Luftwaffe was able to operate in support of the Army to a greater extent and at an earlier stage than anticipated. From the first day of the campaign Polish troop movements came under systematic air bombardment. Attacks were directed at rail depots, loading [and unloading] operations and interdiction points along the traffic routes. Some Polish units were unable to move at all.

The destruction of the Vistula river bridges [and ferries] prevented the withdrawal of the Polish forces and made possible a large-scale battle of envelopment. Tactical air support units made continuous attacks on the retreating Polish forces and this greatly assisted German troops to advance rapidly. The air units supported ground forces fighting their way through the enemy fortified lines. They broke up enemy troop concentrations, pockets of resistance and Polish units spearheading attacks. These operations were closely coordinated with those by the ground forces.

The large-scale attacks by Air Fleets 1 and 4 on Warsaw on 15 September 1939 broke the defenders' will to resist. This brought the 'Battle for Poland' to a speedy conclusion. Thus, Luftwaffe operations made a decisive contribution to the victory in Poland. The success was due to the following factors:

1. the surprise effect of the attacks;
2. properly planned mass attacks by concentrated forces;
3. the lack of proper planning of air operations by the Poles;
4. German superiority in manpower and matériel.

The Campaign in the West, 1940

The study by the Military History Division of the Luftwaffe on the 1940 campaign in the West stated:

With the opening on the campaign against Holland, Belgium and France on 10 May 1940, our Air Force in the West . . . [was] committed in new offensive operations. From experience, its assigned mission included the following tasks:

a. Destruction of the enemy air forces and their infrastructure.

b. Indirect and direct support of army operations.

c. Attacks on enemy ports and shipping.

Air Fleets 2 and 3 were responsible for accomplishing these missions. The actual strength of the Luftwaffe at that time was 5,142 aircraft. Of those, 3,824 were in combat-ready condition, comprising 1,665 [single-engine and twin-engine] fighters, 1,120 [twin-engine] bombers, 342 dive-bombers, 42 ground-attack aircraft, 501 [long-range] reconnaissance aircraft and 154 seaplanes.[3] The opposing air forces (including the Belgian and the Dutch), had a total of approximately 6,000 aircraft, of which about 3,000 were based on Continental airfields.[4]

At the beginning of the campaign the main emphasis was on attacks on airfields in Belgium, Holland and northern France. These destroyed the Belgian and Dutch Air Forces and seriously weakened the Franco-British air forces. As a result the Luftwaffe rapidly secured air supremacy, which allowed it to give increased support to the ground forces. The airborne operations in Holland and Belgium, a new form of warfare, assisted German ground forces to make rapid advances. Once the enemy air forces had been defeated, the demoralising effect of the dive-bomber attacks had a decisive influence on ground operations. Indeed, the drive to the Channel was made possible by the use of large-scale air reconnaissance to screen both of its flanks. This was coupled with a heavy commitment to make use of air power whenever a threat developed. The impression of invincible German air superiority made an important psychological contribution to the breaking of the French will to continue the struggle.

Moreover, the Luftwaffe did not neglect the war at sea. Bomber operations reached their high point during the envelopment of the pocket at Dunkirk. During the evacuation enemy naval and merchant ships came under continuous attack from bombs and mines.

The Balkan Campaign

With the opening of the Balkan campaign in April 1941, the emphasis in Luftwaffe air operations shifted from Western to South-Eastern Europe. The mission directive for the Luftwaffe during this campaign required:

1. effective support for the ground forces through air attacks on the battlefield rear areas;

2. an airborne assault operation to capture the island of Crete.

In February 1941 Yugoslavia had a total of 357 aircraft suitable for military operations. Of these 154 were fighters, 177 were bombers and 32 were reconnaissance aircraft.[5] To counter these, Air Fleet 4 had seven single-engine fighter Gruppen plus three Staffeln, two twin-engine fighter Gruppen, two twin-engine bomber Gruppen, seven dive-bomber Gruppen and a long-range reconnaissance Staffel [a total of just under a thousand combat aircraft, excluding short-range reconnaissance units assigned to the Army].[6]

Facing numerically weak enemy air forces, Air Fleet 4 had uncontested air supremacy from the outset. Thus it could secure quick and decisive results during the campaigns in Yugoslavia and Greece.

For the operation to seize Crete there was neither tactical nor operational surprise. Here again the success of the airborne operation depended on the possession of air superiority. This operation succeeded through the commitment of paratroop forces and [air-transported] mountain infantry units. Other contributing factors were the support provided by the air transport Gruppen, and the attacks by tactical units of Air Corps VIII.

The Russian Campaign
THE EASTERN THEATRE IN 1941

According to experience, the operational plans for the Luftwaffe established the following air missions:

1. the destruction of the enemy air forces;
2. support for the Army by attacks on enemy road and rail traffic, and by direct support over the battlefield.

Air Fleets 1, 2 and 4, and part of Air Fleet 5, were assigned to these missions. At the time the Luftwaffe had a total strength of 5,892 aircraft, of which 3,701 were available for operations.[7] The units committed in the Eastern Theatre had a total strength of 2,150 first-line aircraft. These were divided into 19 single-engine and two twin-engine fighter Gruppen, 31 bomber, eight dive-bomber and one ground-attack Gruppen and 21 long-range reconnaissance and 51 tactical reconnaissance Staffeln.[8]

From radio intercepts it was assumed that the Soviet Air Force had twice as many aircraft [as the Luftwaffe]. In a very short time, however, it was clear from recorded losses that the opposing air force had been much stronger. For the first time the Luftwaffe had entered a campaign in which it was numerically inferior to its foe.

Throwing in everything it had, the Luftwaffe launched a massive surprise attack on the Russian Air Force. By the evening of the second day the Soviets had lost 2,582 aircraft.[9] On the German side it was thought that this would create parity in air power. Then the bomber units were committed in support of the ground forces and made a large contribution to the success achieved on the ground. Air strikes were directed primarily at traffic installations and highways in the enemy rear. The aim was to prevent enemy forces withdrawing and re-establishing themselves behind the Dnieper and Dvina rivers. During the envelopment battles that followed the aim of the Luftwaffe was to prevent enemy forces outside the pocket relieving those trapped inside it, and frustrate attempts by those in the pocket to fight their way out.

However, even during the period June to December 1941 the Luftwaffe was unable to establish continuous air supremacy. The frequent movement of units [and high sortie rates], combined with resupply difficulties, resulted in a serious weakening of the force. The Soviet losses were heavy, but not so heavy as to bring the campaign to an end. Although the Luftwaffe destroyed [huge numbers of] Soviet aircraft it was unable to neutralise the Soviet Air Force. The Luftwaffe had too few aircraft available to furnish air support at all of the points where it was required.

Indeed, 1941 took a course that was to prove fateful for the Luftwaffe. The huge operational theatre in the East, and the [numerical] superiority of the enemy ground forces, forced the Luftwaffe to operate almost exclusively in support of the Army. Yet, if this demand was met, there were insufficient air units to attack targets whose destruction might have reduced the Russian numerical superiority, for example the large Soviet tank factories.

In a wartime study, the Military History Division of the Luftwaffe discussed this subject in some detail. Even in 1941, the outstanding feature of air operations in the East was the preponderance of missions in support of the Army. Indeed, it soon became clear that the German ground forces, confronted with an enemy superior in numbers, could make good progress only when the Luftwaffe supported their attacks. In recognition of this Hitler ordered that large-scale Army operations should be initiated only when the Luftwaffe could offer full-scale support. This order, coupled with the mobile warfare that prevailed up to November 1941, required the commitment of almost all air units to Army support. Only weak elements were left for 'missions of a strategic nature'. The study concluded that if the number of missions flown against Moscow was compared with the size of the Anglo-American bombing effort against Germany, the [much weaker] Luftwaffe strategic air attacks could not be expected to produce decisive results.[10]

Similar circumstances prevailed with the rail interdiction operations. In view of the widely spread Soviet rail system and its low capacity, the German High Command had expected the attacks to achieve decisive results. Here again, however, the available forces proved far too small for the size of the mission. Admittedly, during the first few weeks of the campaign the German rail interdiction attacks caused considerable disruption. This was particularly so during the large encirclement battles. Yet the hoped-for lasting results failed to materialise. The effects of the rail interdiction attacks were localised and, more important, they were temporary. The Soviets developed an unexpected and astonishing talent for effecting rapid repairs. They positioned anti-aircraft guns to defend rail depots, even the small ones. In addition they mounted anti-aircraft guns on trains and stationed fighter units along the routes.

The Luftwaffe fighter force also discovered that it was not strong enough to secure air superiority, much less air supremacy, over the enormous expanse of the Eastern Theatre. This was so despite the superiority of the German fighter force over its Soviet equivalent in terms of training, combat morale and equipment quality. Only by concentrating fighter units over the main areas of ground operations was it possible to achieve local and temporary air supremacy. Other parts of the theatre had to be left without fighter protection. German troops, judging the situation from their limited viewpoint, began to complain that the Soviets had secured air superiority.

Assisted by deliveries of aircraft from the Anglo-Americans, the Soviet aircraft industry replaced the losses suffered at the beginning of the campaign in an astonishingly short time. This enabled the Soviets to resume air activity, though it was restricted to actions close to the battle front in support of ground forces. Only rarely would the Soviets mount air attacks on targets in the German far rear areas, and the Soviet High Command refrained altogether from strategic bombing attacks.

German reconnaissance operations suffered from the same disability, of having forces that were inadequate for the task. This applied particularly to the long-range reconnaissance missions, where the main emphasis was on rail reconnaissance. Had the aircraft been available, it would have been desirable to patrol the entire length of the main rail routes at least twice a day. To find the traffic passing through the larger rail depots, it was desirable to photograph these at least once a day. The lack of sufficient reconnaissance planes made these things impossible. Had such reconnaissance been available, the High Command could have determined whether the traffic observed was for normal purposes, or whether a large troop movement was in progress. In the event, owing to the inadequate reconnaissance force, it was possible to observe only a relatively small part of the enemy rail system.

Anti-aircraft artillery operations were also rendered difficult by the huge expanses on the Eastern Front. It was possible to provide a concentrated anti-aircraft defence at only a few potential targets at any time. The usual pattern of anti-aircraft artillery operations was as follows. Units were sited to defend potential targets near the battle front such as troop concentrations, artillery positions and bridges. These units were also used to engage ground targets such as bunkers, strongpoints and attacking Soviet tanks. Also, air fleet headquarters allocated anti-aircraft artillery units to defend airfields, traffic centres and important supply depots.

The Air Signal Corps experienced difficulties in establishing communications, again because of the great distances involved. Radio communications played an important role. But since these were liable to interference and could be picked up by the enemy, it was not possible to rely on these alone. It was essential for the higher-level headquarters to communicate by teletype and telephone. To give an idea of the distances involved, the landline connecting the Air Fleet 2 command train with Air Corps VIII headquarters was 780 miles long. It was impossible to provide an aircraft reporting network covering the whole vast area of the Eastern Theatre. The best that could be done was to move aircraft reporting [i.e. radar] units to the areas of main air activity.

The air signal-liaison detachments operating close to the front gave valuable service. Reports from these detachments enabled the tactical air support commands to keep abreast of the rapidly changing situation on the ground, and furnished the data necessary for the effective control of combat units.

Logistics on the Eastern Front presented the greatest difficulties of all. Not only were there immense distances to cover, but many roads were substandard and became unusable during the muddy season. This raised problems that often could only be solved only by using air transport. The needs of this front led to significant developments in this area. In August 1941 a Gigant [Messerschmitt 321] freight glider carrying 11 tons of bombs landed for the first time on an Air Fleet 2 airfield. Later a powered version of this glider was built [the Messerschmitt 323], fitted with six engines.[11] Air transport was used by both the Luftwaffe and the Army, and was particularly useful for carrying fuel and ammunition to armoured units that had outrun their supplies during a rapid ground advance.

As the war in the East continued, the position of the Luftwaffe became increasingly difficult. Before the end of 1941 it had been compelled to give up any chance of conducting strategic operations, in order to furnish adequate air support for the Army.

THE EASTERN THEATRE IN 1942–44

From 1942 the pattern of Luftwaffe operations in the Eastern Theatre did not allow a counter-air campaign and army support operations to run simultaneously. The correlation between air operations and ground operations superseded all else. Usually the mission directive for each air fleet required that its air support operations be coordinated with those of a specified army group.

In June 1942 the Luftwaffe had a total strength of 4,264 aircraft available for combat, divided as follows: 1,253 single-engine and 278 twin-engine fighters, 1,237 multi-engine bombers, 369 dive-bombers, 486 [long-range] reconnaissance aircraft, 529 transport planes and 112 seaplanes.[12] During the year the combined combat strength of units committed in the Eastern Theatre fluctuated between 2,000 and 3,000 aircraft.

By then the Soviet Air Force had recovered from the defeat it had suffered in 1941. It was now stronger than before, and it had more modern aircraft. Moreover, the standard of training of its personnel was comparable with that in the Luftwaffe. During 1942 the Soviets restored their force to about 5,000 combat aircraft.

During 1942 the main factor determining Luftwaffe operations in the East was the need to support the large-scale ground advances towards the Volga river and the Caucasus area. The vast majority of air operations were army support missions against targets directly in front of German ground forces. These involved about eighty per cent of the effort of the bomber force. Only small numbers of bombers were committed against targets in the far enemy rear, in actions commensurate with the actual mission assignment.

Strategic air attacks took place only in the central and northern areas, where the [more static] ground situation allowed this.[13] The targets were militarily important industrial installations in the areas around Gorki, Rybinsk, Moscow and Leningrad, the ports of Murmansk and Arkhangel'sk and the railway system.

The Luftwaffe High Command realised the harmful effects of the system in which air operations were tied too closely to army operations. As a result, during 1943 there was a struggle in command circles for authorisation to employ the bomber force in strategic air attacks. At times of little ground activity bombers were sent to attack the giant tank production complex at Gorki and the Jaroslavl rubber plant. Following the opening of the Soviet summer offensive, however, all available units again went into action in direct support of the Army. In 1943 about 80 per cent of all air activities [on the Eastern Front] had been related to the provision of tactical support for the Army.

In 1944 Air Corps IV received orders to resume attacks on communications targets in the enemy far rear and good results were achieved. However, for most of the time it still operated in direct support of the ground forces which, as in 1943, involved 80 per cent of air activity on the Eastern Front.

A study prepared in 1944 by the Military History Division of the Luftwaffe[14] summarised this change:

> The air war after 1941 was characterised by the fact that the Luftwaffe was no longer able to concentrate its activities on one front against one enemy. It was employed in several theatres simultaneously, and had to dispatch forces against the enemy in widely separated areas. This necessarily resulted in a reduction in the strength of the forces at individual sectors on each front. The departure from the principles of air warfare, in favour of providing direct air support for the Army and the Navy, had became an accomplished fact.

Thanks to its inferior strength, the Luftwaffe had to give up its proper role of strategic air operations. This was despite the clear realisation of the adverse results that would follow. Not in Russia, nor in the Mediterranean nor in the Western Theatres could the Luftwaffe hold air superiority. As a result, in these theatres the initiative passed to the enemy and our air force was thrown on to the defensive.

Despite this situation, there were some attempts to achieve lasting results by launching strategic air attacks. Bombers attacked militarily important plants at Gorki, Jaroslavl, Rybinsk, Moscow and Leningrad. No telling results were achieved, however, because the forces involved were too small and the interval between attacks was too large. Due to the difficult situation on the ground, all available air units had to be thrown into action in direct support of the Army. In consequence, units could not be brought into action against lucrative targets such as troop concentrations in the enemy rear. On the enemy side the flow of men and materials into the battle area continued almost without hindrance to create the conditions necessary for their military success.

Notes to Chapter 5

1. Information for this chapter is taken largely from studies prepared during World War II by the Military History Division (8th) of the Luftwaffe.

2. This includes only the strength of units under the Commander-in-Chief Luftwaffe and does not include reconnaissance and liaison units allocated to the Army. The forces under the CinC Luftwaffe were organised under the two Air Fleets [1 and 4]: ten single-engine and twin-engine fighter Gruppen, twenty-one bomber and eight and a half dive-bomber Gruppen, and eight strategic reconnaissance Staffeln.

3. Figures taken from a compilation prepared by the Supply Branch, from unit strength reports.

4. 'Air Power in the West' (1940), article in the Russian newspaper *Krasnaya Swesia* (*Zvesda?*), 14 August 1940. Source No. 206, Division VIa (Foreign Press), Luftwaffe General Staff.

5. 'Umfang und Auswirkung der Unterstuetzung des Heeres durch die deutsche Luftwaffe auf den Ablauf der verschiedensten Feldzuege' (Size and Effect of Ground Support by the Luftwaffe in the Launching of the Various Campaigns), from a study of the 8th Division of the Luftwaffe. Karlsruhe Document Collection, F III 1. Hereafter listed as 'Umfang und Auswirkung'

6. Ibid.

7. This average operable strength of 3,701 aircraft comprised 1,271 single-engine and 130 twin-engine fighters, 1,030 multi-engine bombers, 302 dive-bombers, 593 long-range reconnaissance aircraft, 231 transport planes and 144 seaplanes.

8. 'Umfang und Auswirkung'.

9. Editor's note: 'We succeeded in gaining air supremacy in the first two days, helped by excellent air photography. Reports of enemy aircraft destroyed in the air or on the ground totalled 2,500, a figure which the Reichsmarschall [Goering] at first refused to believe. But when he checked up after our advance he told us our claim was 200 or 300 more than the actual figure' (Field Marshal Albert Kesselring, *Kesselring: A Soldier's Record* [New York, 1954], p. 98).

10. 'Die wichtigsten allgemeinen Einsatzerfahrungen des Jahres 1941' (The Most Important Operational Experiences of 1941), prepared by the Military History Division (8th), Luftwaffe General Staff, Karlsruhe Document Collection, G VI 3a.

11. The Messerschmitt 321 heavy transport glider was originally developed as a means of delivering heavy weapons during airborne assault operations and could carry a payload of up to 22 tons. Initially the normal operational method of towing this aircraft was by using three Messerschmitt 110 twin-engine fighters. Although useful as a means of delivering supplies to forward troops in an emergency, a fully loaded Me 321 needed a lengthy concrete runway to get airborne. The Me 323 was the powered version of the glider. The first heavy-lift air transport in the world, the Me 323 entered service with the Luftwaffe at the end of 1942 and gave excellent service.—A.P.

12. Figures taken from a compilation prepared by the Supply Branch, from unit strength reports.

13. Only a few such attacks were carried out.

14. 'Einsatz zur unterstuetzung des Heeres an der Ostfront' (Operations in Support of the Army in the Eastern Theatre), Karlsruhe Document Collection.

CHAPTER 6

To Sum Up

To an extent it was unavoidable that the Luftwaffe would be required to provide direct support for the Army. In ground operations there were occasions when a critical situation developed that could be relieved only by air power. During a decisive ground battle it was undoubtedly sound practice to employ the bulk of available air units to support the Army. The use of air power in that way established the pattern for the victorious campaigns in Poland in 1939, in France in 1940 and in the Balkans in 1941.

Generally speaking, the same held true for the first few months of the war on the Eastern Front. Yet the continuing use of air power to support the Army, during the periods of relative quiet that followed each great land battle, was not a sound policy. Air Field Manual No. 16 stipulated that attacks on enemy military resources, with operations to establish and maintain air superiority, were the primary missions of air power. And, the Manual went on, this should remain the case unless or until large ground forces were locked in decisive battle with the enemy.

The German High Command and the Luftwaffe High Command ignored these doctrines, particularly during the campaign on the Eastern Front. Once the Russian numerical superiority in tanks and ground-attack aircraft had become evident, attacks on the factories producing these weapons would have had a greater impact on ground operations than direct support missions for the Army. This was particularly so when the latter were flown with inappropriate types of aircraft or weapons.

Obviously the Luftwaffe appreciated the disadvantages of the course it was forced to take. A letter sent from the Luftwaffe Operations Staff in November 1943 observed:

1. During the Russian campaign, German air power was employed properly until the German advance reached the Dnieper river line in the autumn of 1941. The destruction of the Russian air forces, and the direct air support given to the [German] ground forces, made possible the rapid advance. From then on, at least part of the Luftwaffe should have been committed in action:

   a. Against rail routes deep in the Russian interior, particularly to disrupt the evacuation of the armament industry to the Russian rear.

b. Against those armament factories within striking range [of German bombers].[1]

After reviewing the reasons why the weaknesses of German ground forces made such air operations impossible, the writer commented: 'we missed some very good opportunities'.

In 1943 several bomber Gruppen withdrew from the line and began training for strategic air operations. In cooperation with the Minister for Armament and Ammunition, a plan was drawn up for the attack on Soviet industry and the supply depots. The plan stated that, by careful selection of targets, it would be possible to reduce the monthly Russian deliveries to the front by 3,500 tanks and 3,000 aircraft.[2] Air Corps IV, with three bomber and several twin-engine fighter Gruppen, completed its training in the middle of 1944. By then the opportunity [to achieve decisive results] had passed, however. What had been practicable was no longer so, for the front line had been pushed so far west that most of the targets were out of range. The lack of a long-range bomber force was acutely felt. Moreover, considering the unfavourable military situation that developed in 1944, the withdrawal of those bomber Gruppen from combat had served only to accelerate the losses in territory.

Obviously the Luftwaffe alone could not solve the problem. The Wehrmacht High Command should have taken stringent measures to increase the strength of the Army [or build up reserves], so that it did not need to rely on continuous support from the Luftwaffe. It was essential to restore to the Luftwaffe its freedom of action, but exactly the opposite happened.

The weakness of the Army in the winter of 1941–1942 was cited as a reason why no Air Force units were available for strategic air attacks on the Eastern Front. Another reason was Hitler's refusal, against the advice of experienced Army commanders, to allow forces to withdraw to a shorter line that was easier to defend [and thus free forces to create effective reserves]. Even after the autumn of 1943, by which time German offensive operations had ceased on the Eastern Front, straightening the front line would still have been a most effective way to economise in forces. Writing on this subject, Captain Harry Butcher, General Eisenhower's aide, observed in January 1944:

The length of the front line in Russia as measured on the map is slightly more than 1,900 miles, an increase of 500 miles over the front line as it existed when the Russians started their big offensive in July 1943. If the Germans retreat to the shortest line from the Baltic to the Black Sea, it is presumed German divisions may be released and the same strength of opposition continued against the Russians.[3]

Yet Hitler refused to yield voluntarily a single yard of territory on the Eastern Front. Instead, he insisted on holding on to frontages that the available German forces could not defend. When German troops went into retreat, time and again he ordered them to hold on to fortified points as islands of resistance in the midst of enemy-held territory. It was alleged this would tie down enemy forces and slow their main advance, yet hundreds of thousands of German troops were lost in this way. Hitler even refused to consider plans for offensive operations that involved an initial voluntary tactical withdrawal. From the summer of 1943 that made it impossible to operate against the Soviets, since the overextended frontages prevented any release of forces for offensive operations.

In World War I the Russian forces were also greatly superior in numbers to those of the German Army on the Eastern Front. Yet a study of German operations during that conflict shows that commanders achieved several decisive victories in operations staged after withdrawals. By banning any such withdrawals, even if they were combined with attacks, Hitler robbed German field commanders of the chance to inflict decisive blows on the Russian forces. Also he exposed his own, numerically far weaker forces to certain annihilation.

The Luftwaffe command organisation was another factor that contributed to the mis-employment of German air power. Each air fleet headquarters controlled its own strategic, tactical and air defence forces, and their ground service organisations. And each air fleet supported an army group. This worked well while Germany fought only on one front, the air fleets operated from bases in Germany and the Luftwaffe held air superiority. Once the conflict developed into a multi-front war, with air fleets committed far inside enemy territory after air superiority had been lost, the system no longer functioned.

During the campaigns in Poland in 1939 and Western Europe in 1940, the bomber units had been concentrated under two air fleet headquarters. Now they were distributed among six air fleets, an arrangement that made a proper concentration impossible. Also, as mentioned previously, each air fleet was harnessed to an army group. This, inevitably, led to bombers being committed continuously and often unwisely in army support missions. By splitting up the bomber force, the Wehrmacht High Command, the highest level of the German military command, deprived itself of an immensely powerful weapon.

After 1941 it would have been wise to withdraw the bomber Gruppen from individual air fleets and place them in a centralised bomber command. That was the only way to secure a concentration [for operations] against a point of decisive importance to the Army. Had this been done, the Luftwaffe would again have been able to exercise decisive influence on military events.

That said, it is not intended to gloss over the huge disparity between the Luftwaffe [and the combined strength of the opposing air forces]. Once the conflict developed into a multi-front war, and the Western Allies deployed their [own huge air] forces, the Luftwaffe was no longer powerful enough to operate effectively.

Notes to Chapter 6

1. The complete text is in Appendix 36 in unpublished appendices of USAF Historical Study No. 163, Karlsruhe Document Collection.
2. These figures for lost Russian production are wildly optimistic. Moreover, to suggest that they could have been repeated month after month borders on fantasy. The RAF and the USAAF strategic bomber forces were far larger, far better equipped and immeasurably better resourced than any such force the Luftwaffe could have fielded. Yet although the Allied bombers mounted numerous powerful attacks on German industrial centres over a lengthy period, they failed to reduce production by an amount comparable with that suggested in the German plan.—A.P.
3. Captain Harry C. Butcher, *My Three Years With Eisenhower* (New York, 1946), p. 483.

Comparative Ranks

Luftwaffe	Royal Air Force	USAAF
Generalfeldmarschall	Marshal of the RAF	–
Generaloberst	Air Chief Marshal	General (4 star)
General der Flieger	Air Marshal	General (3 star)
Generalleutnant	Air Vice-Marshal	General (2 star)
Generalmajor	Air Commodore	General (1 star)
Oberst	Group Captain	Colonel
Oberstleutnant	Wing Commander	Lieutenant-Colonel
Major	Squadron Leader	Major
Hauptmann	Flight Lieutenant	Captain
Oberleutnant	Flying Officer	1st Lieutenant
Leutnant	Pilot Officer	2nd Lieutenant
Stabsfeldwebel	Warrant Officer	Warrant Officer
Oberfeldwebel	Flight Sergeant	Master Sergeant
Feldwebel	Sergeant	Technical Sergeant
Unteroffizier	Corporal	Staff Sergeant
Obergefreiter	Leading Aircraftman	Corporal
Gefreiter	Aircraftman First Class	Private First Class
Flieger	Aircraftman Second Class	Private Second Class

Organisation and Designation of Luftwaffe Flying Units

The Staffel

The Staffel (plural Staffeln) was the smallest combat flying unit in general use in the Luftwaffe. During the early part of the war it had a nominal strength of nine aircraft. Later in the war the strength of a Staffel could be much greater or smaller, depending on the role of the unit and the supply of aircraft and crews.

The Gruppe

The Gruppe (plural Gruppen) was the basic flying unit of the Luftwaffe for operational and administrative purposes. Initially it was established at three Staffeln each with nine aircraft, plus a Staff Flight with three, making a nominal strength of 30 aircraft in all. Like the Staffeln, the Gruppen would later have strengths greater or smaller than that depending on circumstances.

The Geschwader

The Geschwader (plural Geschwader) was the largest flying unit in the Luftwaffe to have a fixed nominal strength, initially three Gruppen with a total of 90 aircraft, and a Staff unit of four, to give a nominal strength of 94 aircraft. As in the case of the smaller units, the strength of a Geschwader could be considerably above or below that figure, depending on circumstances. Originally it was intended that the Gruppen of each Geschwader would operate from adjacent airfields, but under the stress of war the idea had often to be abandoned, leaving individual Gruppen to function independently.

Flying Unit Designations.

The individual Staffeln within a Geschwader were designated with arabic numbers, while the Gruppen within the Geschwader were designated with roman numerals. Thus the 1st, 2nd and 3rd Staffeln belonged to the Ist Gruppe, the 4th, 5th and 6th Staffeln belonged to the IInd Gruppe and 7th, 8th and 9th Staffeln belonged to the IIIrd Gruppe.

The role of a Geschwader or an independent Gruppe was indicated in the title: Jagd (abbreviation J) for fighter, Nachtjagd (NJG) for night fighter, Zerstoerer (Z) for twin-engine fighter, Kampf (K) for bomber, Sturzkampf (St) for dive-bomber, Schlacht (S) for ground attack, Aufklaerer (A) for reconnaissance, and Transport (T). The 1st Staffel of fighter Geschwader 54 was 1./Jagdgeschwader 54 and abbreviated as 1./JG 54; the IIIrd Gruppe was abbreviated to III./JG 54.

The Air Corps (Fliegerkorps) and the Air Fleet (Luftflotte)

The Air Corps and the larger Air Fleet varied in size, and the number of Gruppen assigned to them depended on the importance of their assigned operational area.